KU-437-548

Hope on the Dole

Hope on the Dole

TONY WALTER

First published in Great Britain 1985
SPCK
Holy Trinity Church
Marylebone Road
London NW1 4DU

Copyright © J. A. Walter 1985

All rights reserved. No part of this book may be reproduced
or transmitted in any form or by any means, electronic or
mechanical, including photocopying, recording, or by any
information and retrieval system, without permission in
writing from the publisher.

British Library Cataloguing in Publication Data

Walter, J. A.
  Hope on the dole.
  1. Unemployment—Great Britain
  I. Title   II. Society for Promoting Christian Knowledge
  331.13'7941   HD5765.A6

  ISBN 0-281-04173-3

Typeset by Pioneer, East Sussex
Printed in Great Britain by
The Camelot Press Ltd
Southampton

For
'Pete', 'Rhona', 'Jim'
and all the unemployed people
I have been privileged to meet.

Thank you for your laughter
and your hope
even in adversity.

Contents

CONTENTS

CONTENTS

Preface

It is widely believed that many on the dole are on the fiddle, actively pursuing their own interests at the expense of the tax-payer. This book challenges this assertion. It shows how most of the unemployed are actually sentenced to a life of passivity, with every odd stacked against their taking charge of their own lives.

The book goes on to look at several unemployed people who have refused to accept the sentence. They are taking control of their lives again, and turning unemployment into an opportunity. Far from sponging on the nation, they could turn out to be pioneers of the way many of us may have to live in a twenty-first century short of paid work. We shall do well to listen and learn, not condemn. These may be saints, not scroungers.

Many thanks to Joan Oldman for encouraging me to write the book; to those who put me in touch with several who are coping, and some who are thriving, on the dole; to everyone, employed and unemployed, who gave me their time and their trust — I hope I have not failed you. Thank you, Michael LeRoy, for constructive criticism, and thank you, Diana Barlow, for typing the manuscript so cheerfully and efficiently.

Passing references to other studies of work and unemployment are given in full in the section on further reading at the end of the book.

Where government regulations, rates of unemployment benefit or allowances are given, these are correct as at the time of writing but are, of course, liable to change.

November 1984   TONY WALTER

Introduction

Some people on the dole are happy, and I for one am glad.

One is not supposed to say this. Many on the Right feel that the unemployed should be avidly seeking work at all costs, and are furious at the idea of anyone sitting back and enjoying themselves at the taxpayers' expense. It is crucial for the Right's attempt to control the trade unions that every worker be haunted by the spectre of unemployment.

Many on the Left, currently in opposition, will be angry too. Unemployment is the Achilles heel of an otherwise popular government, so it must be exposed as an unmitigated disaster for all to whom it befalls. Anyone who suggests that unemployment is less than a total disaster for both individual and nation is written off as a deserter from the cause.

In this political struggle, truth is the casualty. The story of those who have frankly admitted that they are likely to remain unemployed for the foreseeable future, and who have decided to make the best of it, is simply being suppressed. Instead, we have on the one hand the misleading stories in the gutter press of the unemployed making a fortune on the side or enjoying themselves on the Costa del Dole. And on the other hand, there are the true accounts in *New Society* and elsewhere of the despair and distress of the unemployed: true, but not the whole story.

In this book, I want to complete the story. I want to show why unemployment can be such a deadening experience, yet at the same time how some people have found some kind of personal resurrection through their suffering. This book holds the traditional Christian view of suffering: it is an evil to be fought, yet there is always hope that the individual may find good through it. Losing your job has been likened to a bereavement; yet we know that, though some never recover from a bereavement, many do and sooner or later begin their life again on a new footing. To suppress every rumour of this new life is to condemn the unemployed to despair. I hope therefore that the unemployed, and those many more who fear becoming unemployed, will be among the readers of this book. I hope they will begin to see how they personally may be able to turn the tables on unemployment. More specific guidelines can be found in *The Unemployment Handbook* by Guy Dauncey.

More important still, I hope that those who are happily employed, or married to those who are, or students who expect to be, will also read the book. I aim to show that the reason so few are finding resurrection is not because of their own personal inadequacies, but because of the way British society treats the unemployed. We taxpayers should be ashamed of how we are using the unemployed for our own material and psychological gain, sacrificing them as lambs on the altar of our own sense of well-being. There are important political changes to be made, some of which can be implemented straightaway. Such changes would be to the benefit of us all, for we are all diminished by the way this country treats its unemployed.

Creative unemployment

Unemployment is often referred to as though it were a 'thing'. Two consequences follow. One is that we imagine that all the unemployed go through the same kind of experience. I remember when I was unemployed being the recipient of some well-meant leaflets from the local Job Centre which aimed to help me come to terms with the guilt, anger and depression which I was assumed to be feeling. The leaflets explained how there is a natural series of feelings that the unemployed typically go through, and they reassured me that these reactions are perfectly normal. I was surprised because I had experienced few of these feelings, and certainly not in the so-called normal order! The assumption of the leaflets that unemployment is a thing which triggers a particular series of responses in the individual is widely held. There is, however, very little research evidence that has been collected specifically to test this 'phase' model of unemployment. Most of the references to research may be traced to just one study of Marienthal, a small Austrian town, in the 1930s. You can only generalize from one such study if you have already assumed that unemployment is a 'thing' that does not vary from time to time, from place to place, or from person to person.

Unemployment is not like that. How people respond to not having a paid job varies enormously depending on how they feel about paid work, what their last job was like, how they lost their job, whether being unemployed is deviant or normal in their locality, and so on. Even in Marienthal, a significant minority did not react in the supposedly normal way. Only when we begin to see what a diverse experience unemployment is will we be able to understand how it is that some people, and some communities, are able to cope with it, and some not.

The second consequence of seeing unemployment as a single 'thing' is that people sometimes talk as if it *causes* other things. It is as though the long-term unemployed person is like a billiard ball that has been potted, never to re-emerge onto the baize. We hear of unemployment 'causing' depression, or ill health, or suicide, or crime among young people. The present government responds by denying that such malaises are caused by unemployment.

In a sense, this defence is correct. There is certainly a statistical correlation between unemployment and such malaises, for the unemployed are more likely to suffer these things than the employed. But to say, as do some of the less than academically rigorous, that unemployment *causes* these things is manifestly incorrect, for plenty of unemployed people are law-abiding, in good spirits, in good health and not contemplating suicide. Fewer than in the rest of the population, certainly, but still plenty. In fact, you would need only *one* unemployed person who was not depressed to disprove the assertion that unemployment directly causes depression. Indeed, most studies of the health of recently unemployed people show that while about 25 per cent suffer a marked deterioration in physical and mental health, around 8—10 per cent report an improvement. The word *unemployment* covers a variety of situations which different people experience differently. It is not a 'thing' which clobbers people uniformly.

I will show later in the book how difficult is the situation of most unemployed people, but it does not help them to talk of their personal responses to such difficulties as being *caused* by unemployment, for this reduces them to the status of billiard balls. Because it takes an inhuman image of the human being, it leads to absurd claims which are easily dismissed. Tragically, the very real physical and psychological pains of the unemployed can then also be dismissed.

So if unemployment does not cause the trials and tribulations of the unemployed, what does? To answer this question there is much to be said for looking at those who don't find unemployment a problem. What is different about their situation and their responses? This will surely tell us what it is about unemployment that is not a problem, which will then help us see what *is* the problem. The point of looking carefully at the minority that have come to terms with unemployment, and may even enjoy it, is to help us understand what it is that is so devastating for the majority. Clearly the devastation comes not from unemployment, but from certain common features of unemployment and if we can identify these features then we have taken the first step toward creating a more civilized society.

Let's face it. Neither Left nor Right is likely to abolish unemployment in the next year or two. In the meantime, let's discover which features of unemployment are personally debilitating, and we may discover to our surprise some things that governments of both Left and Right *can* do something about.

The book is not only about the unemployed and what they do. It is also about the reaction of our society to the presence of the unemployed. I remember back in 1978 being called in to see the Unemployment Review Officer; I had been unemployed for a year, and it was his job to pressurize me to lower my sights and accept any job that was going. I stated that, while available for a worthwhile job, I had spent my time most constructively writing some articles and a book, which were more valued than had been my previous work which had cost the taxpayer far more! Why should I take an unskilled job which I'd be miserable in, when there was undoubtedly someone who was unemployed and would love that job? Surely the officer's duties were aimed at denying the possibility of two happy and productive people, and ensuring two miserable people? How therefore could he call himself an official of the *welfare* state? He answered that he knew he couldn't win this argument, but rules were rules and he had to enforce them.

Such is the dis-welfare produced by society's attitude to unemployment. Such attitudes are not limited to officials of the Department of Health and Social Security. Kindly Christian neighbours of mine have expressed similarly punitive comments that, 'Everyone could get a job if they tried', and, 'If someone doesn't want to work, then they should not expect to live off the state'. Any book about attitudes to unemployment is about praise and condemnation, and how we apportion them. Ultimately, it is about how we attempt to justify our existence and create our own salvation at the expense of our fellow human beings. Unemployment is as much theological as political, economic or psychological.

Outline of the book

We cannot begin to understand how our society treats those without paid work until we have some understanding of how it treats those with paid work. In Part One, I look at what is happening to work (chapter 1) and what people feel about work (chapter 2). How people feel about being workless depends on how they feel about being in work.

In Part Two, I look at how the unemployed are treated. What are the facts and figures of unemployment, and what policies are there to deal with it (chapter 3)? How do people feel about the unemployed? What climate of opinion do the unemployed have to live within (chapter 4)? In chapters 5 and 6, I show how official policies, backed by public opinion, require the unemployed either to look actively for paid work or to sit passively at home. Given the lack of paid jobs and the plethora of useful and interesting things to be done that do not pay, or do not pay well enough to get people off the dole, this sentence to passivity is quite crazy. It locks up the talents and happiness of between a tenth and a fifth of the population. It is certainly not a mark of a civilized society, nor of one that is concerned to generate wealth in any true sense.

Clearly, the loss of paid work is not itself the cause of apathy, depression and passivity among the unemployed. After all, people leave their paid jobs to become mothers, pensioners or to go into further education, and not all of them by any means suffer the supposedly dire consequences of being jobless. Indeed, many thrive on their new calling. The problems of the unemployed stem not from being without paid work, but from being unemployed — which is a very special kind of being without paid work that has been invented by highly industrialized and bureaucratized societies such as our own.

In Part Three, I look at those who refuse to accept this sentence to a living death. Who are they? Is their situation unusual? Are their responses unusual? Chapters 8 and 9 identify from them the keys to a full and creative existence while unemployed, from which it is possible to outline simple policy changes that would free many more of the unemployed, and the employed too. Chapter 10 reviews the evidence in slightly more philosophical mood. Chapter 11 suggests the simple political reforms that would release both employed and unemployed more readily to generate wealth, fulfil themselves and serve each other.

A world without work?

There is a vigorous debate about the long-term future of work.

Some experts predict that never again will workers be required in the numbers that have been demanded in these early years, the first two hundred, of the industrial age. A world built on work will no longer require so many to work.

Two reasons are commonly given for this. One is automation, which could dispense with labour on a scale never before known. Though this is not the cause of present mass unemployment, it could mean that future economic expansion will not bring many new jobs. Central Scotland, for example, has recently become Europe's premier manufacturing centre for computers, but still has one of the highest unemployment rates in Britain. The other reason is that the earliest nations to be industrialized, such as Britain, had a virtual monopoly on world trade. This is now broken, as countries that produce raw materials such as oil hold out for a fair price, and other countries such as Taiwan and Korea take over traditional manufacturing industries such as steel and textiles.

Others hope that unemployment is only short term. The Right consider unemployment to be a nasty medicine that the sick patient (the British economy) must swallow quickly if it is to regain long-term health. The Labour Party consider unemployment to be largely the creation of the Right's economic policies, and therefore reversible over the period of the next government. Other optimists point out that the most highly automated society, Japan, has by far the lowest unemployment rate.

The experts and the pundits are not agreed, and the layman may justifiably feel that crystal-gazing is an unreliable business. Certainly there is more to crystal-gazing than meets the eye: politicians surely have an interest in propagating the idea that unemployment is solvable by them, which means solvable in the short term. Professors of futurology and popular writers clearly have an interest in making scary forecasts. The layman, myself included, is left wondering who he may trust.

However, two things are certain. One is that for much of the 1980s there will be high levels of unemployment. It is therefore of the utmost concern, whether we call ourselves a civilized Tory or a civilized Socialist, what the lot of the unemployed is to be. Part Two of this book addresses that question.

The other is that we cannot discount at least the possibility that we may never get back to the low levels of unemployment that we became used to in the 1950s and 1960s. How are we to prepare ourselves as a society for a twenty-first century in which there may be less paid work than people want? Some contingency plans are surely in order.

Who should be drawing up these plans? A new establishment of futurologists seems to be emerging. A mammoth TV debate *Beyond 1984,* conducted on New Year's Day 1984, was typical in whom it looked to for ideas and evidence: an academic economist, a whiz-kid technocrat thriving on the silicon chip, and an 'alternative' ecological writer. More academics (sociologists, political scientists, economic historians), politicians and trade union leaders joined the final round table discussion. Theologians and journalists are also often included in such debates.

Where, though, is the voice of those who in their own lives are having to face up to a present, let alone a future, short of paid work? Where are the voices of the unemployed? It seems to me quite crucial that any debate about a twenty-first century short of work must include the findings of the unemployed as well as the views of academics and other employed people. I hope this book will be a start.

Not only should our society listen to the unemployed, but it should release them from passivity, so that they can actively explore the future on our behalf. Instead of penalizing them for being out of work as we currently do, we should thank them. In the words of one commentator, in a world short of paid work 'anyone actually choosing not to work is probably performing a national service and should be given a medal not a punishment'.[1]

[1] Guy Dauncey, *Nice Work If You Can Get It* (National Extension College 1983), p. 70.

Drop-outs or lookouts?

What little intelligent talk there has been so far about the unemployed as creative explorers of the future has usually come from the alternative press and the Ecology Party.

They are to be thanked for having raised the issue, but unfortunately it is too easy for them to be dismissed. Too many of their examples are of middle-class drop-outs leading a self-sufficient existence in some tumbledown Welsh farmhouse and gaining inspiration from the teachings of esoteric eastern religions. Or if that is too much of a caricature, all their examples have the 'alternative' feel about them. The result is that the vast majority of ordinary British people — *Daily Mail*-reading suburban mums, *Mirror*-reading factory workers, and *Telegraph*-reading bank clerks — simply do not identify with them. The life of the ecological drop-out is simply beyond their ken.

I talked to all the people I knew who were unemployed, and I asked around and had no difficulty finding people who were making a pretty good life out of the dole. Few, if any, are 'alternative' people. None are card-carrying members of the Ecology Party. And none live in tumble-down farmhouses.

They all live in ordinary towns like Aberdeen or Sheffield or Warrington. These lookouts for the future have all gained inspiration from long-established traditions in both working-class and middle-class British culture about the place of work in the life of the individual. This is crucial. We *already have the traditions in our British way of life to face the future,* but somehow ignore them in a false debate between the supposedly traditional values of industry and the new values of the post-industrial age.

That's the good news. The bad news is that many of us may not approve of the traditions I am talking of. They tend to be articulated by those who have all along resisted the taking-over of the whole of life by the cash values of the market place. Who are they? Women, those with 'bad' work habits, the poor, some petty criminals. Dare we look to these, the despised of our society, for guidance?

PART ONE

Work

1 What Is Happening to Work?

People refer to the unemployed as 'out of work', as though paid employment equals work. This common notion has befuddled our thinking about unemployment, just as it has plagued our thinking about employment.

Katharine Whitehorn easily explodes this idea when she observes:

> Work is a four-letter word, which may be why it is used with such amazing restraint. It is not, for example, supposed to apply to the nappy washing, potato peeling, bath cleaning and sewing on of buttons done by women at home, who must be presumed to be indulging in some kind of perverted DIY. If it isn't paid for in cash, then it doesn't count. (*The Observer*, 4 July 1982)

I have yet to come across a satisfactory definition of work, and I don't propose to make a fool of myself by trying to give one. But clearly work is wider than paid employment. If it is not, then what are most of us doing most of the time? Only one-tenth of the total time of the British people is actually spent in paid work, and no one would suggest that the remaining nine-tenths is all play.

We tend to assume that most of us spend a lot of time 'at work', in a paid job. We think it is normal to be employed. Though 76 per cent of those of working age are in the market for paid work, it may come as some surprise to learn that that amounts to only 35 per cent of the total UK population in full-time paid employment, with a further 8 per cent in part-time paid employment. So only 43 per cent, well under half of the British people, are in paid employment, and many of them are employed only part-time.

What are all the others doing with themselves? Women strongly aver that housework is indeed work, and children would be no less insistent that most schoolwork and homework are indeed work and not play. Further, those who are, as they say, gainfully employed hardly spend all their time in their gainful employment. In his book *Small Is Beautiful,* the late E. F. Schumacher calculated that, allowing for holidays, sickness or other absence, only about one-fifth of their total time is spent at the job. Much of what they do in their 'leisure' time — cooking, painting the house, looking after children, travelling to and from work — is indistinguishable from what other people do for pay; it certainly seems odd not to call it work just because the worker is doing it in his or her 'time off'.

The four economies

What seems to distinguish these different types of 'work' is not the activities themselves, for virtually anything may be done either for money or not for money. I have even been paid by the Post Office for sleeping! And lifeboatmen engage in the most taxing work almost for free. What distinguishes different kinds of work is not different kinds of *tasks* but the different kinds of *relationships* within which they are performed. Four may be distinguished:

The formal economy is the world of paid employment. Jobs are performed because someone is prepared to pay someone else to do them. The deal is: work in exchange for cash. Other motives, such as loyalty, self-fulfilment, service or doing someone a good turn, may also abound, but the basic deal is the work/cash contract. If either party breaches this contract, the other party feels he or she has the right to terminate the contract, either by the worker giving in his or her notice, or the employer sacking the worker.

The household economy concerns work done within the home for fellow members of the household, usually spouses, children or parents. This work is done not for money but out of

14

commitment to the other members or to the family unit as such. It may be hoped that adult beneficiaries of such labour will put in as much as they get, but there is no such expectation with children and sick, disabled and elderly adult beneficiaries. So exchange is not central to the household economy, though it may be encouraged.

The informal economy concerns unpaid work for non-family, non-household, people. Examples are: voluntary work, doing a favour for a mate, looking in on the old lady two doors down or cooking dinner for her, swopping garden produce with neighbours, standing in the local election and holding a dinner party. Though some rough element of exchange may exist (as with hostesses who expect their guests to return the dinner invitation or with gardeners and their produce), the dominant relationships are those of friendship, neighbourliness, love, loyalty, generosity and pleasure in sharing; or perhaps of influence, status and power.

The black economy involves paid work that is not declared to the Inland Revenue. The black economy proceeds according to rules that are a mixture of those of the formal and informal economies. Some payment for the job is involved, but this is usually way below the formal market rate not only because of the tax saved but also because the worker is often doing the job partly as a favour, to return a favour, or to lend a helping hand.

These four categories are not all-encompassing and the boundaries may be a little blurred (for example, I'm not sure where schoolwork would fit), but they do clarify what the world of work is all about. In his book, *The Hidden Economy,* Stuart Henry has proposed a slightly different classification, but he has the same intention of distinguishing forms of work by means of the economies in which they take place rather than the tasks involved. He talks of the market economy (proceeding roughly according to the laws of supply and demand), the redistributive economy (tax and welfare), the domestic economy (i.e. the household economy), and the gift economy (informal and black economies).

In my three non-formal economies, there is a rather loose relationship between cash-flow (if any) and the supply/demand of labour. What generally regulates the supply and demand of labour in the non-formal economies is not money, but other factors such as love, duty, loyalty, friendship, influence or prestige. In this very important sense, these non-formal economies are much more *moral* than the a-moral formal economy. Working for money seems to me to be a morally neutral motive, whereas the motives that govern the non-formal economies all lie within the moral sphere.

There is an idea spread abroad that one of the non-formal economies, the black economy, is immoral. It is certainly *illegal* not to declare earnings, and selfish to cheat other taxpayers, but many undeclared earnings also come as a result of motives a good deal more moral than those underlying work in the above-board economy. Occasionally work in the black economy is immoral, say gun-running; but many would consider some work in the formal economy, such as arms production, just as immoral if not more so.

Some writers on the theology of work have argued that the hallmark of work should be service — service to others, to the community, and to God.[1] If one concurs with this, then the fact is that, in Schumacher's phrase, 'good work' is far easier done in the non-formal economies where service is already a dominant motive. It is far more difficult in the formal economy where money rather than service is by definition the guiding lamp.

Changes

Relations between the four economies have changed markedly

---

[1] For example, Paul Tournier, *The Gift of Feeling,* SCM 1981; Paul Marshall *et al., Labour of Love,* Toronto, Wedge, 1980.

over the centuries, and may currently be undergoing another important shift.

In feudal times, most work was done in the household economy. The peasant family worked on the land for itself, with little exchange of money. There was also some non-household, non-cash activity. Some labour (such as military service) was offered as an expression of loyalty to their feudal lord, in return (supposedly!) for his protection. Some labour (the tithe) ended up as a gift to the Church, doubtless with coercion and fear of eternal damnation as dominant motives. A formal cash economy was slowly growing in the towns, but the restrictions on usury indicates that there was disapproval of economic relationships in which profit was the sole motive. This was the age of chivalry and loyalty, power struggles and booty, and what we now recognize as the formal economy was emerging only very slowly on the sidelines.

From the sixteenth century onwards, bourgeois merchants and traders and skilled urban artisans became ever more effective in eroding the old feudal order. The cash economy grew and grew. The enclosures of common land over a period of some three hundred years or more changed the self-sufficient peasant family into landless labourers, seeking unskilled work on someone else's farm or — later — in someone else's factory, in return for a wage. The employer, unlike the feudal lord, had few legal obligations to his workers other than to pay them. With their wages, they then had to buy their food and clothing, or much of it. A landless cottager might be able to keep a pig in the garden and grow some potatoes, but wages were also required if the family was to be fed. One mid-nineteenth-century observer of this process described it as follows:

> The bourgeoisie, wherever it has got the upper hand, has put an end to all feudal, patriarchal, idyllic relations. It has pitilessly torn asunder the motley feudal ties that bound man to his 'natural superiors', and has left remaining no other nexus between man and man than naked self-interest, than

17

callous 'cash payment'. It has drowned the most heavenly ecstasies of religious fervour, of chivalrous enthusiasm, of philistine sentimentalism, in the icy water of egotistical calculation. It has resolved personal work into exchange value, and in place of the numberless chartered freedoms, has set up that single, unconscionable freedom — Free Trade . . .

The bourgeoisie has stripped of its halo every occupation hitherto honoured and looked up to with reverent awe. It has converted the physician, the lawyer, the priest, the poet, the man of science, into paid wage-labourers.[2]

Marx was maybe a little romantic about feudal life, but he correctly identified the shift of activity from the household and informal economies into the formal economy.

The year that Marx wrote this, 1847, was about the time when the formal economy was at its peak. In the rush to convert all activity into formal economic activity, young children as well as women were being converted into wage-labourers, and legislation to limit the hours children could work was only just being introduced. Some upper-middle-class Christian philanthropists were getting concerned about women and children becoming wage slaves as well as men.

Though the philanthropists elevated the ideal of the Christian wife at home looking after the family, saving her man from the evils of the world of wage-labour, in fact many married women still went out to work. There was also a massive demand for single women as maids and nannies. As the middle and upper classes got richer and their houses bigger, they chose to pay for childminding and housework rather than do it all themselves — though this was exactly what they were exhorting working-class women to do. So it was that housework, and for a while childcare, became part of the formal cash economy.

Since the peak of wage-labour in Victorian times, there has been a gradual rediscovery of the value of working in the

[2] Karl Marx and Frederick Engels, *Manifesto of the Communist Party*, 1848.

household economy. With increasing life expectancy, there are more pensioners, and the steady expansion of education has also withdrawn more and more people from formally earning a living. Longer holidays and shorter working hours have had the same effect. These long-term changes have reduced the size of the formal economy in all industrial societies over the past hundred years.

The proportion of women in paid work has gone down and up, and varies from country to country. Wars have brought them out of the home, and peacetime sent them back again. Dr Spock influenced many middle-class mothers, especially in America, to stay at home in the 1950s, but the last twenty years have seen a major re-entry of British women into the market for paid work, though much of this is only part-time. By 1981, 54 per cent of women in Great Britain with dependent children went out to work, as did 68 per cent of those with no dependent children.

In some countries, such as the USA and Canada, the overall labour force (those with paid jobs plus those seeking them) has been increasing faster than the number of paid jobs. In other words, unemployment there is not due overall to fewer jobs, but to more people wanting jobs. This is not the case in Britain. In the period June 1979 to December 1982, when unemployment soared, the labour force actually fell by 262,000.

Whatever the changes in the numbers of those with and seeking paid work, the trend is for them to work fewer hours in the week, and fewer years in a lifetime. Over the last hundred years, people have spent less and less of their lives working in the formal economy, till we reach the present time when it is around one-tenth. There is no evidence whatever of this trend being reversed, and it is likely that it will continue apace.

Increasingly, what seems to be happening is that people are producing services for themselves within the home, rather than paying someone else to do it for them. They do their own washing with the aid of washing machine and tumble dryer, rather than send it to the laundry or pay a maid to do it. They

19

transport themselves in their motor car, rather than pay someone else to drive them around in a train or a bus. They entertain themselves in front of the TV rather than go out to the cinema. They do-it-themselves, rather than call in the plumber. It is not inconceivable that in the not-too-distant future, they will diagnose their own illnesses using a home computer and TV rather than going to see the doctor, just as many are getting degrees through the Open University rather than at a more highly staffed traditional university.

Jonathan Gershuny, Professor of Sociology at Bath University, has suggested that there are two very straightforward reasons why people choose to produce their own services. One is that employees are no longer prepared to work for starvation wages, so the price of labour is going up. Bus drivers and laundry ladies may not earn a fortune, but they are more expensive than they once were; it costs more now to pay others to service us. The other factor is that the cost of material goods is coming down, so it becomes cheaper to buy our own capital equipment (a car, a washing machine, a TV) and we can now service ourselves efficiently and with good working conditions. As Gershuny puts it, the rational economic person 'will divert his work activities from exclusively earning money to buy services, to a combination of some work for money to buy goods, with some unpaid work, using the goods to produce services for him or herself'. For example, it pays a lot of people to take two weeks off work, buy an aluminium ladder and an electric sander, and redecorate the house, rather than pay a decorator to do it. There is some doubt whether British industry has been investing enough in plant and equipment, but there is no doubt that the British home since 1945 has been investing massively in capital equipment so that more work in the home may be done, and more productively. This is what Gershuny calls the self-service economy.

(This sheds new light on the common charge that ours is a materialistic age that idolizes luxury consumer durables. When these goods are seen not as consumption, but as tools of production, they begin to make rather more sense. The home may not be the playroom of a hedonistic society so much as the factory of a rather industrious society. It also suggests that those critics who feel that we British do not work very hard may be looking in the wrong place. We may not be working so hard in the formal economy, but in the household economy we may be working as hard as ever if not more so. Or rather our *women* are. Of which, much more anon.)

Gershuny argues that people produce their own services within the home rather than paying someone else to service them. Others, such as Ivan Illich and Jeremy Seabrook, would see it rather more tragically. They reckon that we are coming to rely on things (cars, TVs, computers) to do what in times past we did ourselves. So, in this view, the TV replaces not the cinema but the Sunday evening musical soirée around the family piano; the car trip on a public holiday replaces not the charabanc outing but the promenade through the park, chatting to passers-by as we stroll along; the home computer game takes over from children inventing their own games. We are losing our autonomy, our ability to perceive and use our own skills and talents, and becoming ever more dependent on things produced at the whim of a board-meeting in some transnational company.

I suspect there is some truth in both the Gershuny and the Illich/Seabrook arguments. But they do agree that a lot of activity is going on in the home, much of it undoubtedly work. Where they seem to disagree is over whether it is good work or bad work.

So why is unemployment a problem?

There is plenty of work to do, and there are the four economies available in which to do it. Perhaps all that is changing is the amount of work available in the formal economy. If labour in the informal economies is often as productive, and richer in service and self-fulfilment, than labour in the formal economy, then why is unemployment — forced exclusion from the formal economy — a problem?

It is a national *economic* problem because, for some reason unbeknown to all but economists, only labour in the formal cash economy counts in the official measurement of a nation's prosperity. Gross National Product is the sum total of all the cash transactions in a year, so valued goods and services produced in the informal and household economies simply are not counted. Economists are perfectly at liberty to do their sums this way, but it is absurd for politicians to suppose that a prosperous Britain can only be a Britain with a steadily increasing GNP. The oft-quoted example of GNP going down when a man marries his housekeeper, even though the work done remains constant, indicates how crazy are our measures of national prosperity.

It is a *personal* problem in a more real way. Many unemployed men idolize paid work and would not dream of participating in the household economy. Many an unemployed husband sits at home bored all day, while his wife works a seventeen-hour day scurrying around the home. Sharing the workload fairly is both as vital and as rare within the home as it is within the factory. This question of the unemployed man and housework will emerge as one of the main issues to be considered in this book, for it is central to the whole question of why unemployment is a problem.

Married women often take paid work because of a realistic desire to balance up the pressures of working within the home, and to earn extra money. However, they rarely take paid work because of total incompetence at housework, and so they tend to be more adaptable than many men when they become unemployed, though they may have deep regrets about being confined once again to the four walls of the home. Although the common idea that unemployment is not a problem for women is definitely incorrect, it is true to say that far fewer married women than men find themselves totally lost and adrift when unemployed. Perhaps we men could learn from them.

Options

If the future is to be increasingly with the informal and the household economies, then unemployment will cease to be a problem only when the two sources of its being a problem are changed. In other words, economists and personalities will have to change.

Economists and those who listen to them will have to take notice of the very real wealth-creating non-formal economies. However, this is not a book about economics, and this aspect will not be treated here, though chapters 7 and 11 do refer to it.

Persons are what this book is about. Many will have to work in a wider mix of the four economies than they have hitherto been accustomed to. If the work available in the formal economy is less than the amount sought, then there must be some rearrangement of who works where. There are several options:

Work sharing. Given that most work is both rewarding (financially and emotionally) and wearing, both demanded and avoided, surely it should be shared more fairly?

Work in the formal economy provides a wage which in turn provides power and control over one's life, and will continue to be in heavy demand. In the cause of equity, the available work must be shared around more fairly. This means reduced hours, and more time off at those stages in life when there are other things people would rather devote themselves to — such as a new baby, furthering their education or building a house.

As Sheila Rothwell of the Henley Management College puts it, most men's working life will have to become more like that of women: sometimes full-time, sometimes part-time, dipping in and out of paid work, looking after children. Why, after all, is it regarded as healthy for a man to be a slave to a full-time job for forty years? In this, as in so many things, women are perhaps prophets, as Rosemary Ruether has put it.

At any one time, then, this person of the future is likely to be working at different jobs in at least two or three of the four economies. Over a lifetime, he or she will display a pattern of moving out of one economy, into another, and back again. Flexibility will be the watchword. Anyone who wants to leave the formal economy to be involved in the non-formal economies should be free to leave, with adequate financial support from those who enjoy being in the formal economy.

The benefits could be enormous. Housework and childcare could come to be officially treated as serious work. The fuller part played by women in the world of paid work could lead to a civilizing of that world, for it is women who currently seem more in touch with the caring aspects of human nature that men have excluded from paid work. Men and women might come to respect each other more.[3]

These benefits are not automatic. Things could go a lot worse. More and more people could be involved in the household economy, but with no money to buy the capital equipment needed to make *that* world tolerable, and with no increase in status for the houseworker.

The other possibilities all involve responding to unemployment by continuing with full-time paid work as the desirable norm but forcibly excluding ever-expanding groups of people from it. These are the options that our society seems to be pursuing at present, and that the present government is encouraging.

Send women back home 'where they belong' is one such option. This option notes the increase in women in paid work (up from 7.8 million to 10.3 million in the twenty years prior to 1979), at a time when male paid employment was stagnant. In this view, to send women back home would cure unemployment. The advocates of this view presumably note with satisfaction that, although the number of part-time jobs usually taken by

[3] See Tournier, *Gift of Feeling.*

women is still increasing, since 1979 women have been particularly vulnerable to losing their jobs, and many women have recently been debarred from registering as unemployed.

Women lose their jobs more easily for a number of reasons: the ease with which firms shed part-time labour (usually women); the 'last in, first out' principle for choosing who to make redundant (women tend to have worked for a shorter time in a firm than their male colleagues); wives with unemployed husbands often give up their own job (for several reasons explored in chapter 6).

Forcing the elderly and the young out of the labour market is currently being practised. Raising the school-leaving age and encouraging early retirement are major ways the unemployment problem is being 'solved', irrespective of whether the young or the old want to be in paid work.

Allowing unemployment to continue. This option assumes that full-time jobs will continue to be the norm, and unfortunately a substantial minority of seekers after such jobs will not be able to find them. Because full-time paid work remains the norm, the unemployed will continue to be second-class citizens. If unemployment were not so stigmatized, however, it might be possible for some deliberately to choose unemployment.

Who to look to?

The question is, how are people to move into more participation in the non-formal economies and thrive? Assuming some mix of the four options, it is clear that we will do best, as Rothwell urges, by examining the present lives of women and seeing how they thrive on their present mix, and the factors that cause them not to thrive should be avoided in future.

There are other important questions, however. How are those who are forcibly being excluded from paid work coping — the young, the elderly and the unemployed? Like it or not, they

2 How People Feel about Work

Discipline

The pre-industrial peasant worked when work had to be done; the agricultural cycle involved periods of hectic activity, such as harvest, and other periods when work was more leisurely. The peasant also worked when work *could* be done; if the weather was too bad, or the winter night closing in, then work ceased. If there was nothing urgent to be done, the peasant worked when he or she felt like it. So there was always a reason to work, and the pace of work was determined either by the worker or by clearly visible needs such as getting the harvest in while the good weather lasted. In addition there were about 150 saints' days, many of which were taken off. This is not to say that life was easy, but the pace and structure of work was something very different from what we now generally know.

All this posed something of a problem for that new breed in the eighteenth century, the factory owner. He needed people to operate machinery which ran day in, day out, regardless of weather, time of year, or personal inclination. The raw recruit to the factory was notoriously poor material. He or she had little sense of regular clock time, being used to working according to the weather or the cries of the baby. He could see why he had to go on working his own land, but had difficulty understanding why a factory had to make, say, a hundred clocks a week rather than twenty. He did not see why he could not take off various saints' days. From the employer's point of view, he was thoroughly *indisciplined.*

The historian E. P. Thompson described this fifteen years ago in a now well-known article, 'Time, Work-Discipline and Industrial Capitalism'. Before the Industrial Revolution, the rhythm of work was oriented more to task than to time: 'The work pattern was one of alternate bouts of intense labour and of idleness, whenever men were in control of their working lives.'

27

Clearly not the right attitude for operating machinery in a continuous-process factory!

Also there seem to be natural body rhythms. We can pace ourselves according to these when we are in charge of our own working lives — as did the feudal peasant, and as do today's housewife (children permitting), the unemployed West Indian youth, or this self-employed author. While writing this chapter, I'm taking breaks when I feel weary or when there's a natural break, or when someone calls. This is very different from working in a factory where the machine paces you, or in an office with routines imposed by the firm.

How then did the early industrial factory owner get his workers into what are today called 'good work habits', or what Thompson calls 'industrial work-discipline'?

The most brutal method was handed to the factory owner on a plate. Rural yeomen were being dispossessed of their means of subsistence as the commons were enclosed, and they were left with nothing but their labour to sell. The newly enclosed fields were often given over to sheep, which required the work of fewer men than agriculture, and so there was reduced demand for wage labourers in the countryside. Thousands had little option but to move to the factory and simply fit in. This was physical coercion.

There was also a form of mental coercion, in the form of what is now called the work ethic. This was the idea that work is a good thing. Work is what God (or in our more secular age, self-fulfilment) calls us to. Work is enobling, giving a man worth, in the eyes of himself, his family and his neighbours. This idea was preached in Nonconformist pulpits and in popular philosophical tracts handed out by the likes of Samuel Smiles, who elevated the idea of working hard to help yourself and your family.

In case you are under the impression that people have always valued work, the ancient Greeks gave the lie to that idea. According to Hannah Arendt, the Greek citizen was interested in *work* in the sense of works of art, architecture and philosophy. These were durable and public and were a matter of pride.

Labour was something different. Labour was never-ending toil needed to keep body and soul together, the clothing, feeding and housing of human bodies. This was inferior, and was delegated where possible to the inferior castes of women and slaves, so that free citizens could devote themselves to the public arts of politics and philosophy. Labour was hidden out of the way, in the private home. As a consequence, though public Athenian works of architecture like the Parthenon were magnificent, private homes were little more than hovels.

Christianity has generally held to a very different view. It believes the human body to be created by God. Human life is important, and the work involved in sustaining life is not to be denigrated. Note that most labour in most ages has had to do with physical subsistence, so Christianity gives a general okay to labour.

The Christian view has not been entirely constant, however. The medieval church dallied with the Greek elevation of spirit over body; it valued prayer and contemplation more highly than manual labour, while the cash economy of the merchant was considered evil and fit only for Jews. The Protestant reformers valued all kinds of work, though Luther continued to distrust merchants. The Victorians glorified work of almost any kind.

Ethic or imposition?

The Protestant work ethic is often referred to as though for the past couple of centuries most of the peoples of Britain, the USA, Germany and Holland have been driven by an inner compulsion to work, as though they get their self-respect mainly from their work and go to pieces when they are workless.

That has certainly been true of some, especially those who have interesting work of obvious value to others: the dedicated doctor or teacher, for example. There are jobs in heavy industry and mining where strength, skill, courage and teamwork are required, where men also take great pride in the work. The coalminer and the steelworker have such traditions. Until recently, capitalism has needed labour, and labour has been valued. Especially where their work was skilled or dangerous, workers knew they were needed, and gained respect and strength through that knowledge. Indeed, the labour movement is significantly named, for it is founded on the dignity of labour. Just look at the heroic statue of a working man outside the TUC headquarters in London, or the smaller statuettes adorning the lounges of the Sheffield Town Hall.

There has been considerable talk recently, though, about the breakdown of the Protestant work ethic. We British are supposedly losing the will to work. Our unwillingness to put an effort in at work is claimed to be one reason for our losing markets to the supposedly harder-working Japanese, Germans and Americans. Mrs Thatcher has stressed that we need to rediscover 'Victorian values' if the country is to find its feet again, and one Victorian value she has in mind is the work ethic. Some blame the end of the work ethic on the permissive 'sixties and the laid-back values we have inherited from the hippies. Some socialist writers, like Jeremy Seabrook, blame the loss of pride in labour on capitalism's reduced demand *for* labour. Still others argue that we shall have to develop a leisure ethic to motivate us for a coming age of leisure, and they see signs of this already happening; certainly there is talk now of 'education for leisure', something the Victorian schoolmarm would have found unimaginable.

But how many ever actually cherished the Victorian work ethic? Has a myth been concocted by Mrs Thatcher and a few sociologists playing amateur historian? There is considerable evidence that (a) many never held the work ethic in the first place, (b) many of those who did, held it rather lightly — only so long as it was necessary and so long as it suited them, and (c) of those who did or do hold the work ethic, all actually show considerable ambivalence about paid work.

Consider:

Whatever your values, there is no avoiding the fact that much work is tedious, hard or dangerous. Arendt (*The Human*

Condition, p. 48) observes: 'All the European words for "labour", the Latin and English *labor*, the Greek *ponos*, the French *travail*, the German *Arbeit*, signify pain and effort and are also used for birth pangs. *Labor* has the same etymological root as *labare* (to stumble under a burden); *ponos* and *Arbeit* have the same roots as 'poverty' (*penia* in Greek and *Armut* in German).'

In addition to any physical hardships, paid work often involves kowtowing to the boss or fitting in with the ways and routines of the firm. The power exercised by boss or routines over the life of the worker may be way beyond what is necessary for the due execution of the tasks he or she is paid to do. He or she becomes simply part of 'the way things are done around here'. For many people there is often little sense of actually serving anyone through their work. This feeling of being stifled and not being able to control events is one of the main reasons that people opt out of employment and become self-employed. Although it may be more stressful or less profitable, there can be considerable satisfactions from working for oneself instead of for someone else. However, the large scale of industry and bureaucracy requires most workers to work for someone else.

Is it any wonder then that most of us know the Monday morning feeling? Whatever the merits of paid work, there is usually something inside us that is reluctant to go back to it, and justifiably so. Many actually act on this feeling, and have developed a tradition of absenteeism. In the Birmingham area, Saint Monday was regularly taken off well into the nineteenth century, and I know one building worker who regularly takes days off to go fishing. If they can afford it, many choose to take an extra week or two of holiday between jobs. I cannot remember the number of times that I have heard professional friends in relatively satisfying jobs such as teaching, social work and medicine moan about the pressures and conditions of work. Why, after all, do we dream of winning the pools and retiring at thirty? In the words of the Haitian proverb, 'If work were so wonderful, surely the rich would have found a way of keeping it all to themselves.'

31

Who then did hold the work ethic in Victorian times? Many surely took a pride in their work, but that was generally a matter of making the best of a bad job. How many actually *lived* for their work? Certainly not the upper classes, for the very word *gentleman* meant someone with sufficient private income not to have to take paid work. Gentlemen distinguished themselves from the *labouring* classes who had to labour to subsist. It was the rising middle classes who cherished the values of hard work and of getting to the top through their own efforts. They were the ones who valued themselves because of their own efforts at work, whereas the upper and working classes tended to value themselves as members of a class: 'I'm Lord Devonshire's son', 'I may be poor but I'm honest'.

Even the middle classes in Britain aspired to escaping work. Their eventual aim was to give up business and become country gentlemen. They aspired to handing down their hard-won earnings to their children who would then not have to work so hard. It was not unusual for the self-made Victorian man to pay to educate his son, who became a doctor or clergyman; he in turn, having less need to earn, earn, earn, would have offspring who became artists and novelists. Though the grandfather may not have approved of his bohemian grandchildren, he certainly was thankful that his doctor or clergyman son could spend his time serving the community rather than making money.

Some American self-made men are different. Andrew Carnegie gave away his fortune to charity, saying he would rather give his son a curse than a fortune. *That* is the work ethic: to believe work so fundamentally good that you do it for its own sake and not for the money, and the last thing you'd do is relieve your son of a life of toil.

It has even been suggested by some historians that this penchant of the successful English businessman to put his profits into decking out a country house rather than re-investing in his business, this ineradicable weakness of the English to ape its leisured upper class, has long been the cause of our industrial decline; possibly since as long ago as the 1850s when the first generation of grandchildren of the original barons of the Industrial Revolution took charge of the nation's business.

Granted, the Victorian middle class devoted itself to making money in the booming formal economy, but this applied only to adult males. Women and children of all classes were urged to be diligent in their appointed tasks in the household economy, but for them to go out to work was not approved of by the bourgeois guardians of the moral order. Though all were exhorted to work hard and manifest the work ethic, only men were supposed to hold a *paid* work ethic. That is being revived today, with a Prime Minister urging men to work harder in their jobs, and women to go back home to care for sick dependents that the National Health Service can no longer afford to look after.

Resisting wage labour

My argument is beginning to emerge. If we idolize paid work and/or need it in order to subsist, then unemployment is likely to be a personal disaster. But there are many traditions within British culture that do not have this view of paid work in the formal economy. In the words of Ray Pahl, Professor of Sociology at the University of Kent and one of the very few to have carefully studied people's involvement in the informal economy, 'it is important to recognize that the continued resistance to time-disciplined wage labour is a magnificent resource in coping with some aspects of unemployment'. Let's look at some of the commoner ways in which people today live on the basis that wage labour was made for man, not man for wage labour.

Work only when necessary. Most people work mainly for the money. Some people work only when they need money. Some married women get a job only when there is some special item — a new washing machine, a holiday, painting the house — that needs to be paid for. They may work for a few weeks or months, and then return full-time to the household and informal economies. Students use the same criterion for working during vacations, and those working their way around the world work only for as long as is necessary to get them to the next stage of their journey.

Petty thieves may work only when necessary, though for them the need may not be money. It may be necessary to have a job, while on bail prior to a court appearance or on probation, in order to give a good appearance.

Such wives, students or thieves may actually enjoy their paid work, but they do not kid themselves or anyone else that they hold the work ethic. They are not working because of some inner drive, nor in order to earn respect from others.

Work only when enjoyable. Some may have no urgent financial need to get a paid job. They will take a job for a while, though, if it looks interesting. Sometimes the wife in a family where the husband's earnings are adequate may be able to do this. I think of one such woman who works a few weeks a year for the Swiss Milk Marketing Board. Her job is to hold dinner parties and find out what her friends think about milk products, so that the Swiss can gear their advertising toward the British market. She is due to spend a week in the United States to set up a similar programme.

These reasons — enjoyment and interest — for briefly entering the formal economy are precisely the reasons that many people enter the household economy (to have a baby), the informal economy (to do a worthwhile or interesting voluntary job), or the black economy (thieving can be fun). Such people do not work in any of the four economies because of any work ethic, but because they want a life that is enjoyable, interesting and worthwhile, and they move in and out of the four economies as and when opportunities arise. The Milk Marketing Board woman, for example, also has two young children and is a very enthusiastic vegetable gardener (household economy), has written a successful book (self-employment in the formal economy), is training herself to become a garden designer (would lead to full-time employment in the formal economy), and shares some land and livestock with three other couples (informal economy). Crèche facilities are available for the children, so she can choose to scale up or down any of these activities as opportunities arise.

Work in any of the four economies may also be chosen because it is deemed more *moral* as well as more interesting. Many mothers stay at home because they feel it is right, and many husbands go out to work for the same reason.

Stuart Henry in his study of borderline crime, *The Hidden Economy* (Martin Robertson 1978), observes: 'Personal morality rests on doing things to help other people. The result of such reasoning is that a person can arrive at the conviction that part-time crime is actually *more* moral than most legitimate business.' The opportunities for displaying virtues such as loyalty, dependability, courage and unselfishness are generally higher in the thieving community than in most unskilled legitimate jobs. Crime may also be an attractive way of serving one's family. I think of a professional poacher known to a friend of mine who did not want to abandon his alcoholic wife during the hours when drink was available and who had undisciplined step-children requiring more supervision than their mother could give them. Occasional night work on the river was the answer.

I make no judgement here as to whether in some absolute sense it is morally right for mothers to stay at home or for fathers to earn their living by poaching. I am simply noting that the feeling that it is right is what motivates many people to work, in any or all of the four economies.

Semi-employment. Much work is both low paid and not particularly enjoyable. Among the unskilled who, if they followed the paid employment ethic, would be condemning themselves to forty-nine years of unremitting toil for little reward, there is often a tradition of working for a while and then going on to a not very much lower income on the dole for a while. Such a

35

tradition is particularly likely to develop if much of the paid work available is seasonal — hotel work, harvesting, construction — as in the Isle of Sheppey where Pahl did his research. The Aberdeen fish trade has such a tradition among its lower-paid workers.

Choosing to work intermittently is deemed a poor habit by Job Centres and other professional counsellors, and indeed is not much use to employers who want dutiful factory fodder. It is, however, a very rational response to not very encouraging prospects. The West Indian school-leaver who opts for this kind of semi-employment looks at the 64-year-old white street cleaner next door who has dutifully taken the other course and is about to retire on a pension that is less than supplementary benefit; the kid decides that he is not going to sacrifice his life in like manner on the altar of wage slavery, and he has a cultural tradition to back him up in this. If there is good paid work, then the paid work ethic makes sense. But if there is only bad paid work, or (more recently) no paid work, then it is a mug who holds the paid-work ethic. Or so at least many of the semi-employed feel.

Self-employment. Many resent the lack of autonomy at work. Sometimes this resentment leads to industrial sabotage: literally putting a spanner in the works of the production line that is tyrannizing the workers' lives. Or the worker may respond by indulging in a little fiddle and getting some pleasure that this time he's scoring one over the boss.

Others simply move out of the wage-labour market altogether and decide to work for themselves. Autonomy brings responsibility, and with it both pleasure and anxiety. Some find the anxiety too much, and return to the security of having a boss to do the worrying for them. Others thrive, and with time become horrified about the idea of returning to employment. Susan, temporarily unemployed between businesses, went to interviews for typing jobs, but 'the prospect of being ordered around by some incompetent charlie', as she put it, was too much, and she preferred to spend these months with no income and seeing her savings dwindle.

People have their pride, and refusing a paid job as too demeaning is not unusual. Susan certainly holds the work ethic in that she likes to be busy, but she does not hold the paid-employment ethic that a paid job is *per se* good for you. She has unlearned the industrial work-discipline, and is on a par with the 'pre-industrial' West Indian or seasonal fruit-picker who never learned it in the first place.

Counter-culture. Since the 1960s, there seem to have been rather more people with the guts to face up to the fact that the jobs they are offered or trained for do not in any real way fulfil the worker or serve the community, and have decided to work in an alternative way, meeting their own needs for creativity or serving the community. Though some may feel themselves very modern, they are in fact rediscovering some of the pre-industrial values of work. In their effort to be 'alternative', they often unfortunately cut themselves off from the pre-industrial work traditions I have been discussing that have continued right throughout the industrial age to the present time.

When these various traditions are surveyed, it becomes impossible to conclude that everyone in Britain is besotted with the idea of paid employment for its own sake.[1] Many people reckon that other things, though less well paid or not at all paid, are more worth while than the paid jobs on offer. Many people rationally assess whether full-time paid employment for a lifetime is to the benefit of themselves, their families, or their communities. They move in and out of the four economies. Most, but not all, of these people are either women or poor.

---

[1] I now think I overstated the extent of the work ethic in a previous book, *A Long Way From Home* (Paternoster, 1979). However, that book's general critique of idolatry, including the idolatory of work, remains consistent with the theme of the present book.

They articulate human values that do not fit with the official ethic of an industrial society, and the male, employed establishment ignores or trivializes them and what they do. 'And what have *you* been doing today, dear?'

I suspect that many employed men, at heart, actually have mixed feelings about work. True, a recent survey in *The Times* (23 June 1980) found only 4 per cent of employees claimed to 'hate my work', but it seems unlikely that many who choose to or have to spend the best years of their life and the best hours of each day at a demeaning, ill paid or unhealthy job will admit to themselves that it might just all have been a ghastly mistake. It is an admission they are likely to make only when they retire, when their mixed feelings about work emerge in mixed feelings about retirement; they miss their work and their mates and the pay, but they're glad to have given it up and let someone else clog up their lungs with asbestos or coal dust.

Reactions

What is the official reaction to these various traditions of resisting or avoiding wage labour?

As far as married women are concerned, there is no stigma attached to staying at home, indeed it is often encouraged. Marxist writers suggest this is because the mother is engaging in the valuable work of breeding and feeding the workers that the industrial system needs, and doing it, moreover, for free. Though only 10 per cent of women never go back to paid work after childbirth, at any one time as many as a third of married women *without* dependent children do not have paid jobs, but nobody suggests they are sponging off husband or state. Unlike the unemployed they are not cajoled into looking for a paid job. Indeed, some firms prefer male employees to be married, as they then will not be draining their energy washing their own socks and cooking their own meals; in other words the firm gets the wife's labour for free. Some employers, such as the Church of England, have even been known to make a virtue of this.

Sometimes it is expected that the wife will restore the worker emotionally as well as physically after a demanding day at the office or at the operating table.

As far as the self-employed are concerned, they may be free thinkers, but they work hard and approve of business, they pay (most of) their taxes and are not a drain on others (except through the taxes they don't pay), and above all they usually vote Conservative (or possibly SDP). The establishment tolerates the self-employed.

Society reserves its venom for those men, and to a lesser extent young single women, who stick two fingers up at industrial work-discipline. Indeed, so threatening are they to the old industrial order, that there is a fear that anyone who is unemployed (other than a married woman) is, or may turn into, such a decadent creature.

Nowhere is this more clearly seen than in the 'problem' of youth unemployment. Why has this been declared a potential national disaster? Partly out of a very real sympathy for our unemployed children, but also because there is the fear that young people who have never had paid work may never learn 'good', i.e. time disciplined and submissive, work habits. There is the fear that if they do not experience the joys of paid work, they may become so misguided as not to want it. In the words of the *Daily Mail,* they may turn into welfare junkies, unashamedly dependent on 'welfare' paid for by those in work. Hence the plethora of youth training and work-experience programmes, anything to keep them off the streets.

I suspect this fear is grounded more in the anxieties of workers than in the actual behaviour of the young unemployed. Most of them actually do want paid jobs, indeed it is touching how desperately many do, given the lack of paid jobs available. A survey by Golding and Middleton found that young people under 25 experience as much shame and embarrassment at asking for social security as other age groups; indeed, more than some of the over-55s who feel that, after a lifetime of work, they have surely earned their dole. One may also observe that many of those recently retired, bearers of the good old work habits, themselves started their working life by being unemployed in the 1930s, yet are hardly notable for having caught some lifelong antipathy to work!

It seems to me that if there are any who are 'work-shy', then far from being a threat to the old labour-demanding industrial order, they may rather be the saviours of a world with not enough work to go around. Remnants of values and habits from pre-industrial days may yet serve us all in good stead if there is a 'post-industrial' age yet to come.

Moralizing about work

The main purpose of this chapter is to argue that people have mixed feelings about work and that traditions of antipathy to wage labour have persisted right through the industrial age.

A subsidiary point that has emerged is that work is a moral matter. People moralize about work, and about the workless. Some of this derives from deep feelings about both the value and the pain of work. The benefits to both individual and community of work, and the costs of the toil involved, are so huge that we cannot but feel strongly about those who appear not to be contributing to the community through work, or about those who appear to have avoided a life of toil.

Some of our moralizings about work and the workless, however, have less deep roots. Often our morality seems little more than a crude rationalization for economic motives. For example, the right of the disabled to paid work was legislated for in Britain in 1946, a time when there was a massive shortage of labour. Now that there is an over-supply of labour, the disabled are finding it more difficult than ever to find good paid work and their cause is rarely heard. A more well-known example is the civil rights movement in the United States which led to tremendous improvements in the number of blacks employed in good jobs; now with the recession, the 'first-in, last-out' principle means that it is blacks and other recently advanced groups who get made redundant first. The moral principle of civil rights flourishes in an era of full employment; the moral principle of 'first-in, last-out' in a time of recession. The way in which people operate natural justice seems to follow the fortunes of the economy.

An even more instructive example has been pinpointed by Chris Phillipson in his book *Capitalism and the Construction of Old Age* (Macmillan 1982). He shows how ideas about retirement go up and down in time with the national demand for labour. In the 1930s, there was much talk of encouraging older workers to retire early, with one member of the Cabinet subcommittee on pensions going so far as to say that 'A man of sixty who has worked all his life will not suffer much demoralization through living in idleness . . . idleness may be a boon to the old.' The over-60s were selfish to carry on working, and their ability to withstand idleness their greatest asset. By the late 1940s, the moral rhetoric had been completely reversed, as the nation became desperately short of labour in the effort to rebuild a war-shattered Britain. Doubts were expressed as to how the elderly could be supported by a workforce decimated by war; they were described as 'passengers, not crew', dragging down the economy, and were urged to remain at work. Now that in the 1980s they are again not needed in the labour force, there is much talk of an active, purposeful retirement, with pre-retirement education thriving. So much for the rights and duties of the old.

We may feel that our values about work are timeless or God-given, but history often demonstrates otherwise. They shift to suit the economic needs of the time.

Theologians, churchmen, philosophers and other experts on ethics have joined the debate about unemployment and the future of work. This is quite proper, for work is inevitably a subject about which people moralize, and we surely could do with guidance as to how we moralize and pontificate. This chapter suggests two things that professional moralizers should bear in mind.

41

One is to be cautious lest they make too much of values that have arisen out of a particular historical situation and which may be appropriate only to that situation.

The other has to do with the problem of pain. Schumacher has suggested that work has three purposes: to produce valued goods and services, to serve others, and to satisfy the worker. However, even when these positive aspects are present, people may also suffer when they work. Suffering is easier to bear when we can see a meaning for it. Therefore, out of compassion for those who toil, we may collude in inventing meanings for work. Undoubtedly there is a genuine meaning and purpose in much work, but there is also the pressure to create meaning for work that really is meaningless and damaging. I suspect that those who have articulated the work ethic have done so partly out of awareness of the potential goodness of work, but also partly out of the desire to provide comfort for those who, often unnecessarily, suffer greatly through their work.

PART TWO

Sacrificial
Lambs

3   Facts, Figures and Policies

Who are the unemployed?

Who are the unemployed? This is not so simple. Three answers each point to, but do not amount to, an adequate definition of unemployment.

1   Those who draw the dole, that is, those who draw unemployment and/or supplementary benefit who are registered as unemployed. However, this does not include all of:

2   Those registered as unemployed, because not all who are registered are eligible for benefit. Furthermore, though the register is the basis for official calculations of the level of unemployment, it omits many of:

3   Those without paid work in the formal economy who would like to have it. Many of those ineligible for benefit do not bother to register; nor do many whose benefit is too low to be considered worth the hassle; nor do many in the first few weeks of unemployment, thinking they will get a job soon; nor do some who do not want to publicly admit they are unemployed; and many, such as men over sixty and married women, are actively discouraged from registering and are often excluded from official figures of unemployment. Thousands on special schemes for the unemployed are not allowed to register as unemployed even though they are in the market for a properly paid job. In other words, the unemployment register reflects the rules for claiming benefit, not the numbers of those wanting paid jobs.

However, apart from there being no figures on (3) and the difficulties of collecting such figures, there is a problem with defining unemployment as being without paid work and wanting it. This is that, as this book shows, many of the problems reported by the unemployed do not have to do with their lack of a paid job, but with the hassles and restrictions that are imposed on those who draw the dole. Those in categories (3) and (2) who do not draw the dole do not suffer many of the classic pains reported by the unemployed.

A further problem with definition (3) is that some people inevitably give up wanting paid work when it is not available. Over-sixties, who in more buoyant times would be looking for work, may now consider themselves prematurely retired. Thus the proportion of men aged 60—64 who have withdrawn from the labour force has steadily increased in recent years as the recession has deepened:

$$1975 — 18 \text{ per cent}$$
$$1979 — 27 \text{ per cent}$$
$$1980 — 40 \text{ per cent}$$

Likewise some married women who would be looking for work in better times have at present withdrawn themselves from the labour market.

Not to realize this is to become over optimistic about the ease with which unemployment can be reduced. For the official rate of unemployment to be reduced by, say, one million, considerably more than one million jobs will have to be found. That is because (a) some of these jobs will be taken by currently unregistered women and by men in their sixties, and (b) as unemployment begins to drop, some people in these groups will start registering as unemployed again.

This leaves us with the official register (2), but there is a further drawback with this. Not only does it not include many of those who would like paid work; it also includes a significant number who (arguably wisely) are not looking for paid work.

This complex situation may be simply represented as two overlapping circles (see diagram). The darker area (those wanting a job and on the dole) represents the obviously unemployed, while the two lighter areas (those wanting a job but not on the dole, and those on the dole but not looking for a job) also represent unemployed people who might well move into the darker area should the economy improve or social security

THE FOUR MILLION UNEMPLOYED

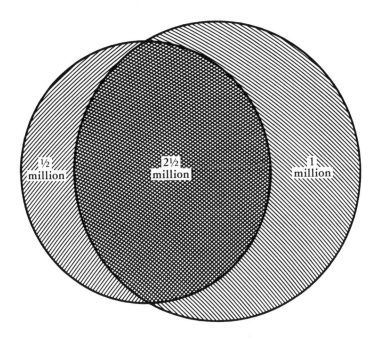

½ million

2½ million

1 million

KEY

 Those on the dole

 Those actively seeking paid work

(Numbers in each segment are the author's estimates.)

regulations change. These lighter areas do not necessarily entail a less serious situation — some of the unemployed ineligible for dole are in desperate financial straits — and all in the lighter areas suffer some of the pressures of unemployment.

However, the official register — listing those without paid work and drawing the dole — form the only readily available figures, and I am forced to use them. Few who have studied the figures deny that they seriously underestimate the numbers of those who would like paid work in the formal economy were it available.

The facts

How many? For the twenty years prior to 1967, unemployment stayed at around 300,000 or 1.5 per cent of the labour force. It was not a public issue, as 1.5 per cent was assumed to represent an acceptable time-lag for those changing jobs. In the late 1960s, it rose to 2.5 per cent. In 1972 it reached 3.7 per cent, but inflationary policies of the then Prime Minister, Edward Heath, quickly brought it back down again to 2.6 per cent. Then began a slow but steady rise, levelling off for a while in the last two years of the Wilson/Callaghan government:

> 1975 — 4.1 per cent
> 1976 — 5.6 per cent
> 1977 — 6.0 per cent
> 1978 — 6.0 per cent
> 1979 — 5.6 per cent

At the beginning of 1980, the unemployment rate began to shoot up, reaching two million in November 1980, three million in September 1982, and is now widely considered Britain's number one problem:

> 1980 — 7.3 per cent
> 1981 — 10.4 per cent
> 1982 — 12.1 per cent
> 1983 — 12.9 per cent

Though unemployment is certainly connected to the international recession, its course has varied considerably from country to country. Throughout the 1970s, unemployment in Britain was about average by European and North American standards. Indeed, until 1978 it was considerably lower than the North American rates. Only in 1980 did the UK level dramatically soar above those of countries with whom it had for years been keeping company. By January 1984 the rates for some major countries were as follows:

Great Britain	13.6 per cent
France	9.3 per cent
USA	8.0 per cent
Germany	7.1 per cent
Sweden	3.2 per cent
Japan	2.8 per cent

The British rate is still well below the 20 per cent of the early 1930s. However in several areas it is over 20 per cent, and over 30 per cent in one or two parts of Northern Ireland. Several housing estates of 50,000 souls, as big as a fair-sized town, have a male unemployment rate of 40 per cent, and a youth unemployment rate of 70 per cent. It is not unusual for a man to have less than half his acquaintances employed.

Although there are now around three million unemployed in Britain at any one time, considerably more experience unemployment in a year. Also at any one time there are many more than three million affected by unemployment: either trying to recoup a standard of living that fell when recently unemployed, or having to take a job at a lower wage than they have been used to, or unable to move jobs or locality.

How long? The average period out of work is about six months. However, this conceals a wide variation, for 1.2 million have been out of work for more than a year, and 600,000 for over two years (April 1984). These numbers will rise higher still.

How poor? As the recession deepened, attention began to be paid to the new phenomenon of unemployment among the professional and business classes. However, although they usually shout louder than most, it is entirely erroneous to suppose that unemployment is now evenly distributed up and down the social ladder. Overwhelmingly, the unemployed have had, and are looking for, poorly paid jobs, and the problems of unemployment are to a large extent the problems of having to live on not very much money.

Since there are considerably better chances of getting re-employed for those in the professional and business class, and because they are likely to have the financial cushion of savings in the fewer than average months they have been unemployed, it is not uncommon for middle-class people who have experienced unemployment to be relatively unsympathetic to the long-term unemployed. Often they retort: 'I managed to find a job without much difficulty', 'I was not short of money'.

Adrian Sinfield has pointed to some important differences between unemployment in the United States and in Britain. In the States, it is much more widely distributed among the income groups. It is also much more likely to be short-term: in 1979/80, the United States had much the same unemployment rate as the UK, but only one-ninth of its unemployed had been out of work for more than six months, whereas one-third of ours had. In the United States, unemployment is far more likely to strike middle-income people and be short-term, which may have fostered the American recognition that it exists and that it is manageable. In Britain, though, there is an enormous gulf of experience between the many lower-income people on the dole for long periods and those who run the country, who may well not know even one unemployed person. This presumably helps foster the polarized attitudes of those who have long proclaimed unemployment to be a national disaster, and middle-class voters and their MPs who — until recently — have simply ignored it. Their attitudes are rooted in fundamentally different experiences.

Why work? There is a widespread belief among those who have not been unemployed that social security benefits are too high, leading to a life of luxury on the dole which saps the motivation to return to work. What are the facts?

A single person receives when unemployed on average only 25 per cent of his net income when in paid work; a couple with two children aged three and six, 55 per cent; and a couple with four children aged three, six, eleven and sixteen, still only 65 per cent. In May 1983, one quarter of those receiving unemployment benefit needed to have it topped up with supplementary benefit, because it left them below the official poverty line; and 12 per cent of those registered as unemployed received no benefit of any kind. The vast majority of people on the dole experience severely curtailed finances. Only 3 per cent get more in benefits than their net income would be if they had a paid job, and they are among the poorest people in our country. Many of those who would get more on the dole nevertheless choose to take or stay in paid work. In fact, in the UK, unemployment benefit is currently at virtually the lowest level compared with average take-home pay for twenty years, yet unemployment is at its highest levels.

A recent United Nations survey shows that the gap in the UK between incomes in and out of work is much bigger than in most other Western European countries, yet they have much less unemployment. It concludes that benefit levels have had little to do with the rise of unemployment in the UK.

A recent survey commissioned by the government and carried out by the Policy Studies Institute discovered that 'the benefits to wages ratio appeared to have no influence upon the time given to job seeking, nor to the frequency of job application, nor to refusal of job offers.' This study found that those receiving higher levels of benefit — notably men with families — tended to apply for more, rather than less, jobs. Similar research carried out by other government agencies such as the Department of Health and Social Security (DHSS) and the Manpower Services

Commission (MSC) points to the same conclusion. It is now quite clear that those who continue to assert that benefits on the dole sap the will to work do so on the basis of dogma, not evidence.

Professor Patrick Minford of Liverpool University argues that, once travel and other expenses of going to work are taken into account, the minority who are better off unemployed is not insignificant, and benefits in excess of net wages are a major cause of unemployment. However, his calculations about expenses have been challenged,[1] and his whole argument is based on how rational economic man would behave in this situation, a dubious substitute for empirical studies of how people actually behave. Minford goes on to argue that benefits act as a 'floor' for wages, below which employers cannot find people willing to work. If this is the case, then the solution is surely to follow the example of our successful European competitors and raise wages, not to lower benefits as he suggests. Or, as I argue in my last chapter, devise a social security system that does not penalize work.

The only people who, research suggests, may often be deterred from finding paid work because of the relation of benefits to wages are women with long-term unemployed husbands. Wages from the part-time, low-paying work, which such women usually do, would be less than, and therefore deducted from, their husbands' supplementary benefit. This is one of several reasons why women with unemployed husbands are markedly less likely to have paid work than those with employed husbands. In such a doubly unemployed household, both husband and wife benefit from the same social security payment, yet typically one (the wife) is deterred from seeking work, while the other (the man) is not. What deters her is not high benefits but low wages.

[1] See Davies, Minford and Sprague, 'The IFS Position on Unemployment Benefit', and a reply by Kay and Morris, in *Fiscal Studies,* 4 (1), 1983, pp. 66—79.

As will be discussed later in more detail, there are also very real ways in which *higher* benefits would aid job-seeking. Due to low income, the unemployed are far less likely than the employed to have a car, a telephone and a new suit, all of which help considerably in finding a job. Urged to 'get on their bikes' to seek work, the fact is that the areas of high employment, south-east England and Aberdeen, are considerably beyond biking distance for the majority of the unemployed, who happen to live in the Midlands, the north of England and the south of Scotland, not to mention Northern Ireland. The unsuccessful executive applicant will be paid his travelling and hotel expenses for a job interview in Aberdeen, but this is far less likely for an unsuccessful blue collar applicant. (He may get financial help from the government's Job Search Scheme, but only after meeting all thirteen of its eligibility rules.) For the family scraping by from week to week on social security, there simply is not the spare cash to send the husband off to Aberdeen or London for a fortnight to look for work. In other words, it takes money to get a job.

There is therefore considerable evidence that benefits deter effective job seeking because they are too low, evidence having to do with the economic facts of job seeking. There is very little evidence that benefits generally deter job seeking because they are too high.

Where are the unemployed? The unemployed are distributed unevenly not only among income groups, but also among different parts of the country and different parts of any one city. National, regional, and even city averages mask areas of extremely high unemployment. Since the unemployed are likely to live in such areas, it is extremely difficult for them to find a job without having to move house. Or put another way, there are some areas where there is relatively little unemployment and those with jobs may even be able to change jobs with relative ease; and there are other areas where those without jobs cannot find them.

'On yer bike'? On the surface, Norman Tebbitt's advice to 'get on yer bike' to look further afield for work sounds good sense. However, even if they can afford to go far in search of work, many unemployed think twice about doing so, and with good reason.

One reason has to do with housing. From a village where the coal mine has recently closed and where you have to sell your three-bedroom terraced house for only £8,000, moving to London where comparable accommodation costs at least £35,000, or to Aberdeen where it is £50,000, is not a recipe for economic solvency. Council house transfers can be difficult when moving out of an area with no jobs, while the few booming areas are likely to have a long waiting list for council houses.

Another fact of moving long distances is that you cut yourself off from friends and relatives. Should you then get laid off from your new job, as is not unlikely (witness Corby or Invergordon where new steel and aluminium works were hailed as economic saviours for migrants from depressed areas in the 1960s and closed down a few years later), you are then cut off from those who can provide both emotional support and the informal social networks through which most blue-collar jobs are found. In the long run, you could well have had more chance of finding a job through the old contacts and knowledge of the local labour market back home.

The Bishop of Liverpool has questioned the moral wisdom of 'getting on yer bike'; he claims it leaves behind the inadequate and less adventurous, as the natural leaders of a community go away in search of greener pastures. Inner-city areas thus become communities of the left-behind. Evidence is mounting that moving may not even be *economically* wise for those who try it. One researcher in South Wales informed me that very few are migrating out of this depressed area in search of jobs elsewhere, because they know perfectly well that their prospects elsewhere are little better; the West Midlands, the traditional destination of unemployed Welshmen, now has as much unemployment as South Wales. It may be that those who leave are now not the natural leaders but the inadequates. Certainly one lady who sells houses on a new development in Wiltshire tells me she has a steady trickle of redundant steel workers coming from South Wales to investigate whether it is worth moving; typically, they are not the Bishop's 'natural leaders' but confused, ill-informed and unhappy people who are not even aware of relative house prices or the impossibility of getting a mortgage while unemployed.

So much for the 'who, when and where?' of unemployment. What policies are there at present regarding those who find themselves numbered among the unemployed?

Policies

All British governments to date have claimed that they have the tools to reduce unemployment to acceptable levels. Clearly it would be electorally risky not to claim this.

The present Labour opposition, like the Labour administration of 1974—9, advocates among other things directly providing jobs through expanding the public sector. The present Conservative government has rejected this option, and is going instead for a general economic recovery in the private sector. It therefore has no policy of helping the unemployed person directly by funding new jobs.

Since, like its predecessors, the present government is optimistic about the prospects for national economic recovery, none of its policies for the unemployed recognize the possibility that unemployment may be here to stay. Claiming that work is just around the corner, it is therefore concerned with preparing the unemployed for the upturn when it comes. Leaving aside general policies for economic recovery, what policies are there specifically for the unemployed?

(In addition to the national policies described here, there are also initiatives by local authorities aimed at increasing employment in their area. These can vary widely. The Department of Employment in Leeds, for example, encourages the setting up of small businesses, while West Midlands considers that a more effective way of increasing employment is to put money into established businesses which happen to be going through a lean patch. Differences arise not only from differences in philosophy, but also from varying local conditions and the kinds of business likely to thrive in a particular area. The local picture is too complex to sketch here.)

Help with finding a job. The government considers that the first duty of the unemployed is to look for a paid job. Benefit is payable only if you are 'available for work'. Each town has a Job Centre which carries adverts for jobs, most of which are local. Unemployed professionals and executives are put on the Professional and Executive Register (PER) and are eligible for a rather more sophisticated counselling and job advisory service.

Job Centres are usually markedly short of customers, compared to the social security office where the unemployed have to sign on each week or fortnight. This is not because the unemployed are not looking for paid work. It is because they have a realistic assessment of the chances of finding a job through the Job Centre. Many jobs have always been found through informal grapevines, knocking on doors, being a friend or relative of an existing employee, or drinking in the pub and finding out what's going. 'I got the apprenticeship through my uncle who works in the same firm.' As the recession has deepened, employers have often not needed to advertise in the Job Centre or local paper because they or their employees already knew a suitable candidate. Why advertise and have the bother of sorting through three hundred applicants when you already know a suitable person?

There is also central government help available for those unemployed who set out on the road of self-employment. If you start a new business, the first few months are unlikely to produce a living wage. If you have been unemployed, however, payment of social security benefits will cease forthwith, because you are now in business and no longer 'available for work', leaving you without an income; savings are likely to have been whittled away by the exigencies of living on the dole. So the unemployed are deterred from becoming self-employed. Under the Enterprise Allowance Scheme, if you are receiving social security and have been unemployed for thirteen weeks or more, have £1,000 to invest in your business, and the proposed business is approved by the Manpower Services Commission (MSC), then you may be eligible for free counselling and an allowance of £40 a week for the next fifty-two weeks to compensate for the loss of benefit.

The aim of this scheme is to get people off the unemployment register. Though advertised as helping to set up 'small' businesses, it does not help the very smallest business — the unemployed man who cleans windows a couple of days a week, the woman who supplements her income by a little typing work at home, the out-of-work academic who manages to get occasional consultancy work. These *really* small businesses are, for reasons to be explored in chapter 5, actively discouraged and pushed into the black economy of illegality. For the vast majority of unemployed with less than £1,000 to put into a business, *this* is the only kind of small business open to them. The kind of operation supported by the Enterprise Allowance Scheme may look like a 'small' business to politicians or their advisers in the Confederation of British Industry, but to many of the unemployed it is far too big a business. Despite the rhetoric, they know that the smallest of businesses are officially persecuted.

What about help with finding part-time paid work? There is the Job Splitting Scheme (not to be confused with job sharing), which is supposedly 'designed to help employers split full-time jobs and so open up more part-time jobs for unemployed people'. However, its rules have been so framed that the scheme is not available to most of those actually looking for part-time work, yet is available to those who are not! The scheme is available only to those already in full-time jobs or to those wholly unemployed and receiving unemployment benefit. To receive unemployment benefit you must have to be looking for a *full-time* job, which is why married women seeking part-time work do not receive unemployment benefit, and are barred from registering as unemployed. So the scheme appears to be a device for reducing unemployment statistics, benefiting neither those who want full-time, nor those who want part-time jobs.

Training. A currently fashionable doctrine is that when the international economic upturn arrives, the new jobs will be in the new high technology industries. Therefore, if Britain is to compete successfully, it must have a workforce trained to use this kind of technology. And even now, it is believed that it is in this area that labour is in demand. If there are lots of vacancies in computer programming and lots of unemployed shipbuilders, it should make sense to train the unemployed from the shipyards in computer programming.

So the MSC is funding a whole range of training programmes for the unemployed. Three particular groups of unemployed with unwanted skills have been targeted. There are those made redundant from a declining industry, for whom there are retraining courses of up to a year; there are women who are wanting to return to paid work after some years spent bringing up a family, and who may need retraining in a new line of work or simply need to become aware of the opportunities in today's world of employment; and there are school-leavers with no work skills at all, for whom the Youth Training Scheme (YTS) is supposed to offer training by employers in skills that may be required in future.

The effectiveness of these training programmes has been widely questioned. YTS schemes provide an employer with free inexperienced labour for up to twelve months. Some employers take their responsibilities seriously, but the system is an open invitation to abuse, with the poor lad or lass left with the menial and dirty work. It is true that the old apprenticeship system could also be abused, but employers knew that it was up to them to train the next generation of shipbuilders or watchmakers, without whom there would be no shipbuilding or watchmaking in future.

Secondly, even if training does take place, there is no guarantee that there will be a job to go to at the end of the period, or that employers will recognize the training. I met Jack, an unemployed Sheffield steelworker who had gone on a twelve-month MSC course, retraining as a heating engineer, which he enjoyed. At the end he walked into the Job Centre with his piece of paper, proudly optimistic about getting a job. He became very disillusioned when the Job Centre told him straightaway that he had no chance of getting one, and was amazed to find that employers accepted only time-served apprentices or people with experience. Such an experience is not untypical.

Work experience. There is a limit to how long you can spend pretending to train an unemployed school-leaver of less than average ability. However, it has become a conventional wisdom that it is bad for youngsters to be hanging around with no paid employment (the exception, of course, being young mothers); and it is correctly presumed that employers often discriminate against those with no experience. So there have been developed programmes designed to give unemployed young adults work experience with employers for up to twelve months. As with most training schemes, the young person is paid by the MSC not much more than they would get on the dole; the employer is given free labour at the cost of considerable bureaucratic red tape. The Community Programme, introduced in 1982, pays rather better, but it is still below a living wage for a family. It is addressed to those unemployed for more than six months if aged 18—24 and those unemployed more than twelve months if over 25, and provides them with temporary employment for up to a year on projects of benefit to the community.

The manifest reward of paid work is that you get paid: paid a living wage and a fair reward for the work done. This central experience of work is not a feature of most 'work experience' jobs. Further, the employer need not demand much of the worker because he is not actually paying the worker, and the worker is not sackable. In other words, the basic contract of paid work in a capitalist society, namely that you pay me in return for my labour, is not present. It is therefore not surprising that both employers and youngsters rarely see these as real jobs. Like the training schemes, they are a way of keeping people off the unemployment register.

Work experience and training schemes do not start with questions such as, 'How long does it take to train a word-processor operator?' and 'For how long does our firm require an extra labourer?', and then devise a scheme to meet these needs. Rather, you have to start with the regulations of the MSC concerning eligibility and, above all, the twelve-month period for which the person can be 'employed'. The result is that MSC schemes tend to be very inefficient forms of working and training. Especially is this so of organizations that serve people rather than things. It may not matter too much for an office to have to change its MSC typist every year, but it matters enormously that an old people's welfare organization has to change its MSC organizer every twelve months. Just as the organizer has built up his or her contacts and come to be known and trusted, it is time to hand over to another novice.

It is odd that a government committed to free-market principles should have allowed the growth of such an inefficient way of working. MSC schemes may be cheap on paper, but their real cost in terms of adding less than they could to the wealth of the community is not counted.

Finally, as suggested in the previous chapter, there is no evidence that to go from school straight to several years on the dole is likely to make youngsters permanently workshy. Similar fears of 'apathy and listlessness . . . bred by long periods of unemployment' were expressed by the Unemployment Assistance Board in the depression of the 1930s, yet Adrian Sinfield (in *What Unemployment Means*) has pointed out that by 1944 there was virtually no one not in employment: Leicester had six unemployed recipients of National Assistance, Birmingham eight, and Rugby and Reading had none at all. The evidence seems to be that, however long people have been unemployed, they will take jobs if they are available and pay a decent wage. And if they become more fussy about the quality of work, surely that is to be welcomed?

Motivation. There are various measures to be described in chapter 5 to encourage those on the dole to go back to paid work. Apart from making signing on an unpleasant and often degrading experience, the main measure is the denial to the unemployed of the long-term supplementary benefit rate. Supplementary benefit is available to social security claimants (pensioners, widows, the disabled, the unemployed) whose benefits are not enough to live on. After twelve months, supplementary benefit is increased to a higher level, in order to pay for irregular expenditures that crop up as items such as shoes and spin-dryers wear out, expenditures that can perhaps be avoided for the first few months but not put off forever. The benefit levels are worked out as the minimum necessary for civilized existence in our society.

That the long-term unemployed are the only group denied this civilized minimum is recognized as punitive both by advocates and critics. To make life financially dire for the long-term unemployed is justifiable only on the assumption that to be unemployed for over a year is a sure sign that you cannot really be looking for paid work, and that therefore you need a kick up the pants to re-motivate you. This policy has widespread implicit support from a large number of employed voters who believe that most of the long-term unemployed must be shirkers.

The fact is, though, that there simply are not the jobs to go around. And even if there were, we have already seen that forcing people to live at the breadline makes it *more* difficult for them to find a job elsewhere if there are none available in their local area.

The structure of benefits for the unemployed was devised in

the 1940s on the assumption that henceforth there would always be full employment and that people would be unemployed for only short periods, largely while changing jobs. Unemployment benefit, financed by National Insurance contributions, was offered for up to a year. It was not expected that many would be unemployed for longer, and those who were would be eligible for what is now supplementary benefit once their unemployment benefit had run out. However, as we have seen, there are now over half a million who have been out of work for over *two* years.

Women and the home. There are 8.8 million female and 11.5 million male employees in Great Britain (1983). Of the women, 5 million work full time and 3.8 million part time. Only 0.7 million men work part time. Those who are seeking part-time work cannot register as unemployed and cannot draw unemployment benefit. The many unemployed women seeking part-time work are thus excluded from official figures. Many people think of the unemployed as *men* seeking *full-time* paid work.

There seem to be background assumptions behind these policies and attitudes: that the married woman does not really find unemployment a problem because she has an alternative role to retreat to, that of wife and mother, and that the married man does not have the alternative role of husband and father. This may indeed be what many men and women feel, but the system does not give people the choice, and makes life difficult for those men and women who prefer to work in the 'wrong' one of the four economies.

Whose fault?

All the policies aimed directly at the unemployed make sense only if unemployment is in some way or other the individual's fault. He or she is inexperienced, untrained, or workshy; give him or her work experience, training or a kick up the pants and he or she will be more likely to get a job. Given the verbal recognition by all political parties that unemployment is largely not the individual's fault, it is remarkable that actual policies for the unemployed presume precisely that.

Looked at in the short term, all the present programmes of training and work experience simply give some unemployed people a headstart over others, thus shifting around who has the jobs. It forces people into a kind of pseudo-formal economy, where work is done with neither the humanity of the household and informal economies nor the productivity often associated with a free-market formal economy.

Present policies for the unemployed fail to recognize three things. One is that many of the unemployed want paid work, for which they are trained and have experience, yet will not find it for years. The second is that many women want paid part-time work and this is real work just as much as full-time paid work is. The third is that some of the unemployed do not want paid work, but could become an asset to the community if they were allowed to work productively in one of the non-formal economies; also, they are relieving the pressure for jobs in the formal economy.

In other words, there is lip-service given to the right of men to paid work, but there is uncertainty as to whether women have an equal right and there is certainly no right for men not to seek paid work. The various policies look forward to a future of largely male full-time paid work in the formal economy. That, apparently, is what our society, head in sand, is seeking.

4 The Politics of Righteousness

Attitudes toward the unemployed are often less than charitable. This self-righteousness is significant for three reasons: it provides public support for the policies described in the previous chapter; it creates a climate of hostility and distrust within which all the unemployed have to live to a greater or lesser extent; and it diminishes all of us, employed or unemployed.

Claimant and taxpayer

Around 1976-7 there was a massive attack in the popular press on unemployed social security claimants. There were scary headlines about claimants ripping off the Department of Social Security, claiming under several different names and living a life of leisure normally reserved for pools winners. The idea was also propagated that anyone on the dole, especially those with large families, could live very comfortably off state benefits, and that therefore many were unemployed because they preferred to live a life of affluent indolence on the dole. Taxpayers resented having to pay for these free riders.

This scare helped foster a climate of opinion that unemployment is not such a bad thing and is often a preference of the work-shy. It certainly helped the election in 1979 of a government whose manifesto and campaign virtually ignored unemployment. Though unemployment is now widely recognized as a problem, punitive attitudes and policies still persist.

Attitudes to tax evasion have always been very different. In the public's view tax evasion is rather like driving offences: a technical offence, not one to be ashamed of. But to fiddle the social security is to rob honest you and me, and is a heinous crime. The fiddling taxpayer is just an ordinary mortal, the fiddling claimant is the lowest of the low.

Similarly, legitimately avoiding tax through the good services of a clever accountant is 'okay', but to screw the social security for every penny you are entitled to is the mark of the scrounger. The front page of a Sunday paper once had an advert for tax planning (that is, for a consultant telling you how to avoid tax legitimately) placed by ironical chance next to an article condemning social security scrounging. One suspects that many readers would not have connected the two activities.

Why is there such outrage at the fiddling social security claimant, and why the belief that so many unemployed claimants are on the fiddle? Surely not because of the facts of the matter. In 1977, the Supplementary Benefits Commission estimated that £340 million of benefits were not taken up by people who were entitled to claim them, while in the same year, detected social security fraud was only £2.8 million, or one-thousandth of social security claims. In the same year, the Inland Revenue wrote off ten times that amount of evaded tax as not worth pursuing, even though they could have traced it had they cared to. Estimates of the total of undetected, and largely undetectable, evaded tax at the time ranged from one *thousand* million pounds to *three thousand* million. In 1979, 82 per cent of a group of selected cases of self-employed workers and companies were found to be understating their income for tax purposes. Petty theft runs at around £1 million a day.

Ordinary taxpayers are robbed to a far greater extent by other taxpayers and by petty thieves than they are by fraudulent or work-shy social security claimants. Yet there is no outcry against tax evaders (let alone legitimate tax avoiders) or even against petty thieves. Why? Surely because we are all taxpayers, and do not want the taxman to peer too closely into *our* tax returns. Surely also because many of us have taken materials from work or exaggerated travel expenses to a value equivalent to that of many a convicted petty theft. Many who believe the scrounger myth are themselves robbing Her Majesty's treasury by not declaring income for taxation.

It is easy to see why there is no outcry against tax evasion, but it is less easy to see why there is such strong feeling about unemployed social security claimants. After all, the middle-aged do not complain about paying pensions to the elderly, nor do the childless appear to mind a large part of their rates going to pay for the education of children. Why is there this hostile division between employed taxpayer and unemployed claimant, when it does not exist between other contributors to and beneficiaries of the public purse?

One reason has to do with the principles of our social security system. As I have described in more detail in my book *Fair Shares,* the individual believes that his wages are rightly his because he has earned them, and National Insurance contributions are a way in which he insures against periods of interruption of earnings, such as sickness, unemployment and eventually old age. He therefore feels that he has paid for his own pension, sickness or unemployment benefit, and is pleased to receive it in the knowledge that he has paid for it. He feels entitled to it.

However, our contributory insurance system caters for only one year's unemployment benefit, and even that is often insufficient and has to be topped up with considerable sums of supplementary benefit, which are paid for out of general taxes. Also, since there are many more unemployed than were budgeted for, unemployment benefit is also partly paid for out of general taxes. This is widely known, so that whereas people feel (not entirely correctly) that pensioners have paid for their own pensions, they feel that they are supporting the unemployed. After all, if a worker has paid for his stamp to protect him during his own periods of unemployment, why should he also have to pay for other people who are unemployed out of his general taxes?

Resentment is particularly acute among the low paid. David Donnison, Chairman of the Supplementary Benefits Commission, wrote in 1976:

> Those letters which arrive by the hundred each month, complaining that we hand out too much in social security and support too many layabouts and scroungers, rarely come on

headed notepaper from the leafy suburbs. Most are written by ordinary voters and taxpayers.[1]

Some taxpayers are earning less than some social security claimants they are helping to fund. In this country there has been a dramatic lowering of the tax threshold, the point at which a person starts paying tax. In the mid-1950s, a two-child family would be exempt from income tax until the breadwinner earned the average wage, and then he was taxed at only 9 pence in the pound. Today, tax is payable on earnings of less than half the average wage and starts at 30 pence in the pound, a higher starting rate than every other country except Australia. The great expansion in the welfare state has been paid for not by milking the rich but by taxing wage earners right across the board, which hits the low paid worst of all. The 1974—9 Labour government continued to expand taxation in this way, with the low paid eventually feeling things had gone too far: hence the applause from readers of *The Sun* and *Daily Mail* for their exposés of scrounging, and the election of Mrs Thatcher on a tax-cutting platform with support from the low paid.

Public feeling about the funding of benefits may account for the hostility, but there is then the question of why people feel this way about paying for the *unemployed*? After all, they don't mind paying for health and education, even if they themselves are childless or look after their own bodies assiduously. I suspect this is because health and education are unequivocally felt to be a good thing, whereas people have very mixed feelings about paid work (chapter 2) which get reflected in mixed feelings about those without paid work. Especially do the low paid have mixed feelings about their work.

On the one hand, there is pity for the unemployed, and workers fear that one day they too may be unemployed. On the other hand, there is a part of many a worker that secretly envies the unemployed for having escaped the world of toil. This second bit is getting bigger and bigger as the recession deepens,

[1] *Social Work Today,* vol. 6, no. 20.

for paid work is generally getting worse as a result of unemployment: many workers are now too scared to stand up for their rights or fight for better pay or conditions lest they be dismissed, never to find work again. Others who would normally move jobs regularly as a way of advancement become aware that they are getting trapped in a job that is less than totally rewarding, both financially and emotionally. As paid jobs get less and less rewarding, so does envy toward the unemployed increase.

When I decided to leave academic life ten years ago, at first for a sabbatical on the dole and later emerging into self-employment as a writer, there was considerable interest in my progress from ex-colleagues, specially the married male ones. Part of them admired and envied what I was doing and hoped I succeeded. Another part apparently felt threatened lest I should succeed, and secretly hoped that I wouldn't. This was the time of academic cuts, with virtually no jobs advertised and few opportunities for promotion. Just as they were beginning to feel trapped, so they saw me breaking free. (The female ex-colleagues were largely indifferent. They knew I was only doing what many women do anyway.)

Unemployment is a frightening prospect to most paid workers. It is more comfortable for them to believe that *they* could never become unemployed, and the easiest way to believe this is to believe that people stay out of work only by choice. 'Oh, they could all get work if they really looked,' is a comment I hear around me in my middle-class part of Bath. One defence against anxiety is to focus it on something outside yourself: in this case, to lay the blame fairly and squarely on the unemployed themselves. The unemployed become morally culpable for not looking for work, which reassures the worker that he is right to continue dutifully at t'mill. The one sign of hope is that this kind of projection may lessen in areas of high unemployment where prejudiced views are daily contradicted by acquaintance with unemployed friends, neighbours and relatives who clearly do not fit the scrounger stereotype.

There are three possible explanations for some of those on the dole getting more than some of those in work:

1 Wages are low.
2 Low-wage earners are being taxed.
3 Social security benefits are high.

The first explanation undermines the self-respect of the low-wage earner; it is not nice to know you are being exploited. The second explanation is also depressing for the low earner. The third explanation (which actually has the least supporting evidence) is by far the most comforting for the low earner because it enables depression and anger to be turned outwards.

So it is that the old class divisions are being supplemented by a new division, between earner and claimant. If the next century is to see a very small number of high earners in high technology industries, producing all the goods and services of the formal economy, supporting the rest of us, then current attitudes towards those who are male and fit and adult and supported will lead to a society as bitterly divided as the worst divisions of class war.

In the next section, I want to suggest that antagonistic attitudes toward the unemployed are due not just to present policies and ambivalences about work, but are much more deeply rooted in human, and particularly British, psychology.

Identity

Who am I? All human beings seem to want to answer this question, and there are different ways of arriving at an answer.

One time-honoured method is to identify with the group or tribe to which one belongs. For British people today, this would mean laying some importance on being a Briton, a man or woman, a native of a particular region, or a member of a particular social class.

In our individualistic society, however, people also lay great store by some more particular identification than simple membership of a large group. As affluence spreads, transport, housing and other necessities come to be privately owned by the individual family so that there is less obvious dependence on others. One of the paradoxes of life is that poverty can sometimes be survived by sharing and neighbourliness, which is what traditional working-class culture was all about, whereas affluence can lead to isolation and even selfishness. People still describe themselves as working class, but this is now less to do with real sharing within an identifiable local community and more a rather vague label to do with origins. Certainly affluence is not making the working class bourgeois, but it is breaking a class down into a bunch of rather more private individuals and families. Individual identification is becoming more important.

How then may we identify ourselves individually from others? There are basically two possibilities. One is to relish the relationships I'm involved in, who I am and what I do. The other is to pride myself on what I'm not and who I'm not.

The first method involves gaining self respect from being a good mother, doctor, footballer, welder, pigeon racer, amateur actor or whatever. Some identify themselves more in terms of who they *are* (loyal, caring, ambitious) whereas others, more likely men, have rather poorly developed concepts of who they *are* but have a strong sense of what they *do* and what they are good at. Such people, when asked 'Tell me about yourself?', would reply, 'I'm a time-served fitter/I enjoy playing football/I enjoy work/I race pigeons', rather than 'I'm sensitive/sometimes a bit arrogant/in love'.

The trouble with identifying ourselves in terms of something that we do and are good at is that, in a competitive society such as ours, only a few can be a good footballer or have a prestigious job such as a doctor or nurse or be the best pigeon racer in town. Or our kids may not be behaving themselves too well, and it may be difficult to believe we are good mothers. The difficulty with believing ourselves good, or to be good at things, is that all too often life is rather bad to us. In a competitive society, it is all too easy to feel a failure.

What then? Well, if you cannot succeed legitimately in the race for success, then you might try getting noticed through illegitimate activities. Vandalism, hooliganism and other forms of ostentation are open to everyone.

Most, however, reject this option. Whereas the unsuccessful North American may go on masochistically striving and striving to succeed, ending up possibly in despair or with a broken marriage, we British are more prone to adopt another course. With our finely tuned class system and status distinctions, we can always take pride in looking down on the group below us. I may not be much, but at least I'm better than *him.* We may be a tolerant nation in some ways, but we can also be very censorious of one another.

It is much more comfortable to compare ourselves favourably with someone we consider below ourselves than unfavourably with someone richer and more successful. W. G. Runciman's detailed study, *Relative Deprivation and Social Justice,* suggests that this habit of looking down rather than up may be one reason why the British working class has been more acquiescent than revolutionary. A recent survey by P. Golding and S. Middleton found that *of the poorest third,* only 25 per cent actually recognized themselves as poorer than average, 65 per cent felt themselves about average, and 10 per cent even thought they were better off than average. 'There's worse off than me' is a comforting sentiment that exaggerates awareness of those few worse off, while those much better off are somehow felt to belong to another country and do not count. When asked about the well-off, the low paid refer to miners and car workers, not to doctors or those with inherited wealth. Survey after survey has shown the reluctance of the British poor to admit that they are in fact poor, which surely has something to do with why so many do not claim social security that they are entitled to. That would mean admitting they are poor.

With some of the low paid, the sentiment that 'there's always worse off than us' can be a charitable sentiment, exuding pity for the homeless and disabled whom life has treated badly. But with others, looking down is a self-righteous affair. There is a tradition in Britain several hundred years old of blaming the poor for their poverty. A survey of EEC countries found that nearly twice as many British (27 per cent) said that poverty is due to laziness than does the average European citizen (14 per cent). As Golding and Middleton reported, 'Far more than any other reason, poverty was seen to result from the failure of the poor to control money going *out* of the home, rather than from society's failure to get a decent income *into* the home.'

Traditional views of poverty do not blame *all* the poor. Some are poor by bad luck. They are the honest poor, working hard but limited perhaps by low intelligence or misfortune. Then there are the disreputable poor who are poor because of their own fecklessness, poor housekeeping, gambling, or dislike for hard work. They deserve little sympathy.

This traditional view can be a great comfort to the lowest paid in Britain. Though you may not know anyone worse off financially, it is always possible to convince yourself that there is someone who is not managing their affairs properly, spending what little money they have at the boozer and not looking after their children, or that the blacks have nasty habits and are ruining the country. It is always possible to convince yourself that, even if you are not well off, at least you are respectable.

This is important, because it means that people build an identity by placing themselves not only on the economic ladder, but also on a moral ladder. At all levels of the economic ladder it is possible to feel I am doing well on the moral ladder, and congratulate myself that 'I am good because you are bad'. However, it is when I'm not doing well on the economic ladder that I have most need to feel I'm doing well on the moral ladder, and it is here that the most censorious views of the poor are often found.

The low paid who are committed socialists, however, are more likely to direct their censoriousness upwards — to the bosses, the government or moderate trade union leaders who have sold out. It is arguably healthier for society, and certainly braver for the individual, to direct his or her anger upwards at the powerful than downwards at the powerless.

Folk devils

Constructing a moral inferior is not done by isolated individuals. The mass media and politicians also from time to time create an enemy against which they hope society can unite.

Since the early 1970s I can recall four main public devils. First there was public concern about drug addicts, and especially drug pushers. Rather than facing up to the reality of large numbers of young people taking drugs in a controlled way and introducing them to their friends in much the same fashion that people start to drink or smoke, the myth was created of a small number of evil pushers setting our innocent children on a path to inevitable destruction. If drugs are evil and large numbers of our children are taking them, then it is too much to believe that our children are evil; more comforting to project the evil onto a small number of baddies. This myth was widely believed, even though such big-time pushers were not in fact the main way in which drugs spread.

Moral panic number two was the scare about social security scroungers that peaked in 1976. Here too were identified an evil cadre of those who were out to fiddle the system of as much loot as possible, buying Rolls Royces out of two dozen claims under different names in different social security offices.

In fact, overpayment of benefit is typically made not to a cunning devil but to a confused person in difficult circumstances. There is the unemployed family who provide a temporary roof for a friend or relative in dire need, and fear telling the social security lest an income from rent is assumed, benefit reduced and the lodger forced to go. It is not uncommon for the way the poor share what little they have to disqualify them from benefit, or for them to be so confused by the social security rules that they keep quiet for fear they lose benefit.

Then there was the father of a Sheffield man I interviewed.

He had worked for twenty-five years in the same steelworks, and was then made redundant at the age of fifty-seven. He had never been well paid, but was hard-working and thrifty and had saved £3,000 for himself and his wife in their retirement. After twelve months his unemployment benefit ran out, but he was not eligible for supplementary benefit because of his savings. With another seven years to run before their old age pension would be due, and with no prospect of a job, these savings would clearly be soon whittled away. So he shifted some of the savings into his sister's building society account, and reapplied successfully for supplementary benefit after a few weeks. The assault on his pride after a lifetime of thrift and of being able to support his wife and family was massive. He felt totally betrayed by the system he had worked for all his life. He is not untypical of the person forced to make a slightly false claim to the social security. Last year, when he was 64, he was diagnosed as having cancer of the bowel, and was whisked in for an operation, which seems to have been successful. However, during those traumatic few months, he was informed by the DHSS that he had broken the rules by continuing to register as unemployed (presumably he was not available for work, and should have been registering as sick), and they were considering whether to prosecute him. For several weeks, he and his wife received just a few pounds irregularly every few days until it was sorted out. This again is typical of many 'fraudulent' claims.

But it is not such prosecutions, or near prosecutions, that hit the headlines. It does not make any of us feel good that representatives of our so-called caring society are treating ordinary people like this. If we are to make a god out of our own respectability, then

A poor, witless, bedraggled devil in a struggle against a powerful majestic god makes the god ridiculous. A strong, cunning and powerful devil enhances the power of God. Like any villain, he must be almost equal to the hero if the hero is to gain honor in vanquishing him.

So wrote Hugh Dalziel Duncan in 1962, in *Communication and Social Order,* about the show trials of Stalin and Hitler. Apparently the millions of British who love to loathe the artful scrounger exposed in the gutter press are not immune from a similar mass psychology. Indeed Duncan feels, and I would agree, that Hitler was not an aberration from human nature, but an appalling exaggeration of it; what he appealed to is in all of us. He goes on:

> The fact of victimage, so terribly obvious in our time, must be accepted and studied. Any social theory that does not take into account the terrible fact that men 'need' each other to satisfy their hate, as well as their love, becomes singularly irrelevant to a generation that has lived in the world of Hitler.

The French social theorist and theologian Jacques Ellul, who fought in the Resistance, likewise refers to our apparent need to hate.

The victims of this kind of scapegoating — social security claimants, blacks and others — understand the hate that is in all of us. Only the persecutors can kid themselves that they are good. Many a respectable member of British society does this by means of a double standard. So you find the churchgoer who is genuinely sympathetic to the one or two unemployed people he actually knows, even going out of his way to help them get a job, but is deeply prejudiced against the unemployed in general ('There's plenty of jobs around if you look'). The knowledge that he is genuinely concerned for the one or two enables him to pat himself on the back and remain blind to his general prejudice. If challenged, the one or two are always the 'exception' who really are trying or who have had exceptionally bad luck.

The social scientists, Golding and Middleton, found Duncan's theological analogy appropriate also for describing the reactions of the media, politicians, social security officials and large sections of the public in the late 1970s. In *Images of Welfare* they wrote:

The 'disreputable poor' made the perfect sacrificial scapegoat in a process of social 'redemption through victimage'. The frequently brutal policing of large numbers of claimants has provided 'absolution' of the social order through a colossal ritual purge of the 'guilty'.

As the social security scare began to die down, so the Argies came to the rescue of the frail British personality that seems to need a moral underdog. This was a real war. As in most wars, a complicated and very grey situation with right and wrong on both sides was transformed into democratic St George slaying the totalitarian Argentine dragon. A few of us were worried and not a little scared by what was happening, but in general the British public loved it. Shooting down the Super Etendards out of the sky was even better for the British ego than show trials of social security scroungers. We all, well not quite all, felt very good.

Folk devil number four arrived in the form of one man: Arthur Scargill, leader of the National Union of Mineworkers. The facet of the 1984 coal miners strike stressed in the national press and by the government is not the legitimate worry of the miners over their future livelihood but the moral threat to the nation by a man bent on undermining democracy. Mrs Thatcher even went so far as to compare the strike explicitly with the Falklands War when she described Mr Scargill as 'the enemy within'. Whereas ordinary wars unite a nation against an external enemy, civil wars divide a nation. This particular civil war effectively divided the working class even more than it was already, and may well enhance the chances of the government at the next election even more than the Falklands War did at the last.

In each of these four moral panics, the key has been 'I am good, because you are bad'. What these national panics indicate is that it can be whole nations or large sections of them, and not just individuals, that feel they are not doing well in the economic race and are attracted by looking to the moral rather than the economic ladder for a sense of having made it. Nations as well as individuals try to create their own righteousness.

No work, no worth?

If to be an unemployed social security claimant is to be unworthy and disreputable, how do the long-term unemployed answer the question, 'Who am I?' They surely find it more difficult to find a satisfactory answer than the low-paid worker.

I heard of one redundant steel worker in South Wales who put it particularly well. Being over sixty, he had the option of de-registering as unemployed, in return for which he was eligible for the long-term supplementary benefit rate. He got the money, and the government got one more off the politically embarrassing unemployment register. But he said he feels like writing to Mrs Thatcher to tell her that she has made him officially into a 'non-person': he's not a pensioner, nor employed, nor unemployed. Nor disabled, nor a housewife. He is officially neither in, nor out, of the world of work. But non-persons do not have much self-confidence, and I don't think he ever wrote his letter of protest.

How then does the unemployed become a person? At first it is common to continue defining yourself as a worker. So it is that people who have been unemployed some months may still see themselves as a plasterer or a doctor who happens to be between jobs. That is the real me, whereas unemployment is merely a temporary condition that I happen to be in. It is not *me*.

But after a while, unemployment may begin to get to you. The danger of defining yourself as unemployed is that you take on board the low image that society has of the unemployed. Just as society blames unemployment on the unemployed themselves, so do many of the unemployed. They may feel guilty about not providing properly for their families, or that there is something wrong with them that they are getting turned down for job after job.

However, there is a tradition that can rescue the self-image of the person who has accepted that they are long-term unemployed. That is the distinction between the respectable and disreputable poor. This is turned into a distinction between the reputable and the disreputable unemployed. Even the most adjusted of the unemployed, who have come to terms with their situation and are making a civilized life out of it, had a habit of surprising me by injecting into a relaxed conversation an oddly harsh comment about certain others of the unemployed.

Pete, an amazingly creative single person who brightens up more people's day than most would in a year, has been unemployed the best part of fifteen years, and has the art of living on nothing. He would be embarrassed to hear me say that he reminds me of a modern-day St Francis. Pete is a very unassuming person, *except* when asked about other unemployed people. Then a mild self-righteousness emerges. He says he feels different from most people on the dole, 'Most would rather lie in bed all day than do what I do'. He himself gets up each morning at six and goes on a six-mile run, mainly on what bits of countryside he can find within range of his tower block in a large industrial city. He does this not only because he enjoys it, but also because he fears that if he doesn't get up in the morning, then the brooding and depression will begin. A positive way to start the day, but there is the undercurrent that those who get depressed have only themselves to blame. Of those who find it difficult to manage financially on social security, he says it's their own fault if they cannot manage their money, and in any case there is nothing to stop them getting a job.

John lives in Leeds and is married with two young children. Unemployed for four years and with an epileptic wife, the authorities have allowed him the longer-term rate of supplementary benefit and have accepted that he is not looking for paid work as he is needed at home. They manage, though I have heard it said that he is maybe not as conscientious as he might be in caring for wife or children and spends too long out of the house in political work and doing odd jobs for people. John himself, however, is critical of those unemployed who he sees as not looking after their families properly: 'I've no sympathy for those who spend all their dole at the boozer or bingo and then complain that they've no food in the house.'

Bob Holman, author of the excellent study *Poverty* and a community worker on a somewhat neglected housing estate on the outskirts of Bath, told me how often he has noticed that this kind of bitching among the poor concerns the bringing up of other people's children. One of the problems of being poor in a materialistic society is that it is virtually impossible to bring children up and give them everything that society says they need. Clothing, feeding and caring for children all cost money, and it is generally agreed that social security benefits do not properly take into account the real cost of bringing up children. So, almost inevitably, you have to scrimp on something. The unemployed parent who criticizes another for letting her admittedly well-fed children out looking like ragamuffins is herself criticized by the other for keeping up appearances with good clothes for her children while neglecting to feed them properly. Everyone can find someone who is not doing things right. In fact, I met only one couple who failed to condemn other unemployed couples who chose another way to run their finances: 'It's their choice,' was all they said, tolerantly.

In the next two chapters, I will be arguing that the unemployed are sentenced by social attitudes and policies to sit passively at home. There are few ways they can get satisfaction and a sense of worth for their talents and skills if they are not allowed to exercise them. This leaves many with little option but to pride themselves, in a negative way, that they are not like others. Writers like Bob Holman and Guy Dauncey have argued strongly that it is essential to free the unemployed to exercise their talents and serve others if they are to regain a healthy self respect. One mum, who had been made to feel that she was the dregs, discovered that she had artistic talents that were greatly appreciated by the other better-off mums, from whom she had been isolated before she came to the community centre which drew out her talents.

One result of the backbiting and bitching to which the unemployed are sometimes reduced in order to find some sense of worth is that the unemployed are divided and isolated. They are certainly isolated from the low paid. This is very frustrating for Fred, unemployed and a member of the Communist Party, who spends his time working for the Unemployed Workers Council in his Lancashire town. As he put it, 'We don't belong to any class now'. He understands, as does Mrs Thatcher, that the unemployed will never form a revolutionary class, because they are too divided, too unwilling to accept the label 'unemployed' and act together.

Fred has no derogatory comments about other members of the unemployed, but he has plenty for the DHSS. It's hard to examine your relationship with a more powerful group and come out morally superior, unless you refer to the socialist tradition of 'us the workers versus them the bosses', which is what Fred does. But it seems to me that to villainize the badly paid DHSS clerk who abuses you across the counter in the local social security office, though good for Fred's self respect, is hardly getting to the core of power in our society. The problem for the unemployed is that they are cut off from the mainstream of trade unionism; it is the worker and his labour power that traditionally is the revolutionary force in socialist theory, which hardly leaves any role for the unemployed. They are left fighting their own private battles down at the local pub and local DHSS office.

Social redemption

I have suggested that it is quite appropriate for social scientists to describe the relations between the unemployed and other groups in society in quasi-religious language. Part of the much discussed search for personal identity is what Jacques Ellul has called our need for righteousness, the desire to know that we are right to do as we do and to live as we live. The desire for righteousness that traditional religions address themselves to does not go away simply because a society believes itself to have become more or less secular. Most people still want their lives to be justified. Few indeed can live with the knowledge that their life and works may be arbitrary.

Without a traditional Christian God providing unconditional acceptance, people in Britain today have to create their own righteousness. In this chapter, I have suggested two ways in which we do this: if we cannot create our own righteousness through our own good works, through our own success in a competitive society, then we can create it by taking it out on others ('At least I'm better than him').

It seems to me that the genius of Christianity is the doctrine of the free forgiveness of sin. This enables us to face up to our inadequacies and failures, knowing that we are not blamed for them by God; no longer need we pretend we don't have them or take them out on others. This is an unfashionable doctrine in an age which worships at the altar of human progress. Many do not like the idea of original sin; it's far too negative they say. Much more positive is the notion of human potential. The trouble with this 'optimistic' view is that we have the potential for evil as well as for good, and this potential does not go away simply by ignoring it.

The result of ignoring it is that there is no formal institutional way in which failure may be forgiven and sin redeemed, which is what the Church perhaps once provided. To make up for this, national politics and the mass media have, unbeknown, taken on this task of assuaging guilt. This takes two forms.

The first is the revival by the New Toryism of a secular work ethic in which there are no free lunches and in which everyone has to earn his or her own place in society. This is a kind of Counter Reformation, rebelling against the paternalist welfare consensus of the post-war years that accepted you whoever you were. The New Right finds this offensive, just as the Counter Reformation was offended by Martin Luther's preaching of salvation through God's free grace. Mrs Thatcher appeals to that part of us that likes to earn our own salvation. Indeed, she is popular for precisely the reason that Evangelicalism is unpopular: human pride likes to think it can earn its own way in the world, and is offended by someone else, human or divine, giving us a helping hand.

For the less successful, who find it difficult to save themselves through good works, there is the second means of redemption: the sacrifice of the innocent. People today may find archaic and bizarre the old Jewish practice of making burnt offerings of their animals on an altar, and the Christian development of this idea in its theologizing about Christ's crucifixion, yet the language of sacrifice is commonly applied to the unemployed by politicians today. Unemployment is the temporary sacrifice that we as a society have to make if the economy is to recover, we are told. A burnt offering on the altar of prosperity. But who is it that makes the sacrifice? All of us by cutting working hours? Taxpayers by willingly paying adequate benefits for those who have the misfortune to lose their paid jobs? Not at all. The burden is laid entirely on the unemployed themselves. They are given barely enough, often less than enough, for a civilized existence, under punitive conditions; they are even blamed for their misfortune; and taxpayers then have the nerve to believe *they* are the ones who are suffering through excessive taxation! (Apart from the low paid, the British are not taxed highly by international standards.)

> Upon him was the chastisement that made us whole,
> and with his stripes we are healed. (Isaiah 53.5, RSV)

Isaiah was writing here not just about his own time, nor simply prefiguring the death of Christ; surely he was also describing human nature in which Christ participated, in the role of the innocent who is sacrificed. We participate, through economic policies, political rhetoric and editorials in the *Sun* and *Daily Telegraph,* in turning others, such as the Argentines and the unemployed, into a similar sort of sacrifice for our collective guilt. Rituals of sacrifice are not some strange pastime of primitive peoples. They seem to recur throughout human history. Somehow we feel better by laying all our guilt on an innocent lamb, and then destroying it.

Lambs are particularly helpless:

> He was oppressed, and he was afflicted,
>   yet he opened not his mouth;
> like a lamb that is led to the slaughter,
>   and like a sheep that before its shearers is dumb,
>   so he opened not his mouth.   (Isaiah 53.7, RSV)

In the next two chapters, I aim to show how we render the unemployed helpless. Here the analogy breaks down, for lambs are born helpless. Sacrificial lambs today are not born helpless, they are made so. By us.

5 Sentenced to Idleness (1)

Policies for the unemployed all assume their imminent or eventual return to paid work in the formal economy. The only things the unemployed are officially encouraged to do is to look for a paid job, join officially sponsored substitutes for one, or retrain for one. Many of the unemployed have learned through bitter experience the futility of all this; they know that there is nothing more depressing than chasing after jobs that are not there. Is it any wonder that leaflets handed out by the DHSS warn the unemployed that they may find themselves listless and depressed?

All this is well known. What is less well known is that not only do the unemployed find it difficult entering paid work in the formal economy, but also it is difficult for them to engage actively in the non-formal economies — household, informal and black. They are sentenced to passivity.

In this chapter I will describe the pressures to passivity as they affect all the unemployed. In the following chapter I will deal with pressures which are none the less real for affecting only some of the unemployed.

Lack of money

Just as money is the main thing about paid work for most people so the lack of it is the biggest and most often reported problem of the unemployed.

This need not be true of the first six to twelve months of unemployment. Some find themselves cushioned by redundancy payments or savings, others may decide to cash in occupational pensions. Earnings of up to £2 a day are allowed without unemployment benefit being affected, and a spouse can earn as much as he or she likes. Capital equipment — car, TV and video, washing machine, subscriptions — may be all paid for

84

and in good order. Only after some months do things begin to wear out, clothes need to be bought, and the running costs of car and phone begin to threaten the financial even keel.

After twelve months unemployment benefit is replaced by the means-tested supplementary benefit. Any savings over £3,000 debar you from benefit. You can earn only £4 a week. Any earnings over £4 by your spouse are deducted from your benefit, so he/she may decide to give up work.

Low earners may well face these difficulties from the beginning because of few savings: immediate entitlement to supplementary benefit with the consequent restriction on earnings; and hire purchase commitments which cannot be kept up.

The problems of the unemployed are largely the problems of poverty. The Supplementary Benefits Commission, now the Social Security Advisory Committee, is the body charged by the government to define what counts as poverty in our society in order that it may determine social security benefit rates adequate to keep claimants above the poverty line. Its definition is: 'a standard of living so low that it excludes and isolates people from the rest of the community'. In other words, you cannot send your child to Cubs because there is no way you can afford the uniform. That is poverty.

Some of the better-off may carp that this is not starvation poverty as in India or the Horn of Africa. True. Some of the poor in the non-cash rural areas of the two-thirds world, however, live more purposeful lives than the unemployed in Britain where virtually any activity costs money. Social security scales are calculated to meet *physical* needs. The assumption seems to be that you sit at home, adequately fed and clothed, but with no spare cash for a drink, to order a library book, to go to the swimming baths, to catch a bus to go to church or to a political meeting or to see mother-in-law; and Jimmy certainly can't join the Cubs.

There is a common myth that the unemployed can always earn a little bit on the side, without telling 'the social'.

Considerable hypocrisy lies behind this assertion, because what evidence there is all points to the employed doing more 'moonlighting' than the unemployed. In one survey by *The Economist,* though most of the unemployed shared the belief that casual work was commonplace, only 30 per cent admitted to doing casual jobs and only 8 per cent did so for payment of some kind, and only 4 per cent for cash.

Why should this be? The reason is simple. The same factors that make it difficult for the unemployed to find paid employment or self-employment also make it difficult for them to get paid work in the black economy.

We have seen that getting a job is often difficult without money and resources such as a car and a phone. Let's look at the figures (early 1980s):

Percentage of households with:

	Car	Phone
General population	61	75
Unemployed	38	50
Unemployed more than 2 years	23	30
Unemployed less than 2 months	46	

If you want your house painted for cash, you are more likely to ring up the employed painter and decorator who, you've heard, may oblige than go and call on the address of someone on the dole with no phone who will find it difficult to transport paint and ladders to your house because he has no transport.

That's if he's got a ladder. Moonlighting, like self-employment, requires equipment. The employed moonlighter readily borrows equipment from work. This may be with the boss's consent, as when I worked for a building firm where a perk of the job was to borrow the firm's truck. I'd use it to do a favour for friends, fetching a ton of topsoil or moving a piano, and favours would come my way in return. The employed moonlighter who borrows equipment from the firm, is often not averse to taking materials as well. A piece of wood here, a half-empty pot of paint there, some typing paper. None of this is available to the unemployed entrant to the black economy.

A job in the formal economy has another important advantage. It puts you into daily contact with workmates and customers who also have money. In other words, it puts you in touch with the market for your services. The unemployed person is likely to have fewer social contacts, and — as unemployment tends to cluster into certain districts — several of these may well be unemployed and short of cash also. Areas of high unemployment tend also to have lower than average wages. So there is less cash flowing around, which is bad news for local traders in the formal *and* the black economies.

It is often assumed that, with the increase in part-time paid work for women, a lot of unemployed men cannot be that badly off because their wives are earning. Exactly the opposite is the case. For various reasons to be explored later, the wives of unemployed men are much less likely to have a paid job than the wives of employed men. This also affects the would-be moonlighter, for his wife's contacts at work with other paid workers can be as valuable a source of customers for the moonlighter as his own contacts.

Some of the employed use moonlighting as a way of building up a little business of their own, and eventually becoming legitimately self-employed. This avenue too is much more difficult for the unemployed because of difficulty they have in working on the side.

To summarize. We are becoming two nations. There are those families with two or more earners in the formal economy, either of whom may also be involved in moonlighting. Their job and their wages are what enable moonlighting, which in turn augments their wages. And then there are those families with no earners in either formal or black economy, where the lack of work and money in the formal economy is a main factor in their inability to find work and money in the black economy. The world begins to close in.

Available for work?

If it is difficult for the unemployed usually to be active in the black economy, then what about the informal economy of unpaid work in the local community?

One of the conditions of registering as unemployed and qualifying for social security is that you are available for full-time work immediately should it be offered you. Technically, this means that you cannot commit yourself to any kind of education or voluntary work which you cannot drop immediately if necessary. In practice, the rules for part-time education have been relaxed, so that it is possible for the unemployed to spend up to twenty-one hours a week in further education without losing their benefit. As for informal voluntary work, the picture is confused and variable.

I have come across several examples where the local social security office has tacitly accepted certain claimants doing full-time voluntary work, so long as they can still come into the office at the appointed time once a week or fortnight to sign on. Sometimes the claimant feels that the voluntary work may in due course lead to a full-time paid job. Just as those already with a paid job are more likely than the unemployed to be offered another paid job, so those of the unemployed who are actively engaged in voluntary work may be able to line themselves up for a paid job within the same organization. Jack, previously mentioned, voluntarily did some driving of the minibus that takes old people to a club and on outings, and found himself the obvious candidate when the community organization that owns the bus succeeded in getting MSC funding for a driver for a year.

David is seventeen and left school before completing his 'A' levels because he was unsettled by his father's death. He is going back to college shortly to complete his 'A' levels. In the meantime, he is teaching voluntarily in remedial classes at a local comprehensive school three half-days a week, and from this experience is now aiming at training to become a remedial teacher. He had to change one of his half-days to enable him to sign on at the required time, but otherwise has received no bother from the DHSS.

Sometimes the DHSS approves of full-time work in the household economy. I have already mentioned John, whom the DHSS now accepts is needed full-time by his two young children and partially disabled wife. Unemployed single parents are usually not expected to be available for work, whether they be male or female. However, a girl in Montrose who explained to an official that she didn't turn up to a job interview because her mother was ill and needed looking after was told that was not an adequate excuse — though looking after a sick husband would have been! How the unemployed are supposed to know the mysterious workings of the DHSS mind that says that sick husbands are more in need than sick mothers is not at all clear. In fact, it is precisely this anxiety about not knowing how the DHSS will react to any proposed activity, however legitimate it may seem to the claimant, that leads many claimants either not to do things they would like to, or not to tell 'the social'.

As it happens, the DHSS often is not one hundred per cent keen on voluntary work. Fred, the communist voluntary worker with his own local Unemployed Workers' Council, told me that he is verbally asked each week when he signs on if he has done any work in the past week; he has to sign a statement if he has done voluntary work, and they then check with the organization he has been working for to ensure that no payment has been made. Other voluntary community workers have been made to sign on at different times *every day* so that what the DHSS sees as troublemaking activity may be frustrated. This kind of obstruction of voluntary work cannot happen with the voluntary worker who also has a paid job.

When it decides to, the local DHSS office can make life very difficult. Local councillors, for example, are given an attendance allowance, which is supposed to cover lost wages or other expenses incurred in attending council meetings. One unemployed member of a large city council told me how the DHSS reduced his benefit by the amount of his presumed attendance allowance, and then made him sign on every day for a period of several weeks. At the time he was chairman of housing, and on one famous occasion, when there was a crucial and very narrow vote, there was lengthy fillibustering from his colleagues to give him time to rush back from signing on and to cast his vote. Compare this with the employed chairman of housing in another city; he uses his substantial attendance allowance to fund someone else to do his normal paid job, with the full consent of his employers and no hassle.

There seems to be enormous variation between social security offices as to whether or not voluntary workers receive this kind of hassle or not. I suspect this may be due to the presence or absence of one of the roving special investigation squads which move from office to office, tightening up on social security abuse. They have been greatly strengthened in recent years as the political response to the public hysteria about scroungers. Whether or not they are effective in saving the taxpayer money, they certainly seem to have frustrated some of the good work that is being done by some of the unemployed who have those two rare commodities — time and commitment to their local communities — and who could be of such value in voluntary work and local politics.

Earnings rules

If you are receiving unemployment benefit, you may earn up to £2 a day, and your spouse may earn as much as he/she wishes. If your income (benefit + earnings + child benefit) comes to less than the official poverty level, then you may be eligible for supplementary benefit. Unless you have substantial savings, you will be eligible in any case after twelve months, because unemployment benefit runs out then. On supplementary benefit you may not earn more than £4 a week, except for single parents who may retain half of any earnings between £4 and £20.

Whatever the reasons for these earnings rules, the *effect* is that the unemployed are not encouraged to engage in paid work at the edge of the formal economy. Although the earnings rules are themselves relatively straightforward, they are a part of a whole package of rules for claimants which are very complicated, and some unemployed who are offered part-time work do not take it because they fear that they *may* be breaking the earnings rule or some other rule. Or they take it and keep quiet about it, living in fear of being found out, even though — perhaps unknown to them — they may not be exceeding the earnings limit.

Adrian is an academic and was unemployed for a while between research contracts. He accepted some part-time lecturing because he felt it might lead to contacts and open up some more options, and, being an honest lad, he told the DHSS from whom he was claiming unemployment benefit. This led to endless interviews and negotiations. Because of the complexity of this apparently straightforward strategy to improve his chances of employment, he was paid no benefit for the two months that the DHSS was sorting out his file. Eventually he was paid the benefit he was due, backdated. 'They say you can do part-time work without hassle. It's just not true', was his comment.

Adrian was far from being on the breadline, and had a wife working as a teacher, so he could afford to wait for his benefit; further, being highly educated and knowing his entitlements, he probably got all the benefit he was entitled to and got it sorted out quicker than most. Imagine the situation of those many unemployed who cannot go for two months without income, and who may be less prepared to press for their entitlements. They will either go short, or not tell the DHSS they are working.

The pressures therefore are either to idleness or to dishonesty. Just as lack of a formal paid job makes work in the black economy more difficult, and the 'available for work' rule can create hassle for work in the informal economy, so the earnings rules make paid work at the sidelines of the formal economy less simple.

This is a problem firstly because it takes away from the unemployed the chance to take control of their lives and gain respect by earning a bit extra for themselves or their families. And secondly because, by taking away opportunities for work at the sidelines of the formal economy, it reduces the chances of finding full-time paid work there. Certainly this classic avenue to self-employment is made more difficult for the unemployed. The Enterprise Allowance Scheme (chapter 3) recognizes the problem, but assists only those unemployed who are already willing to commit themselves to self-employment; it does not help those who would just like to test the water by doing a little part-time work on their own account, which for many would-be self-employed is a vital way of testing the market, their own skills and how they react to working for themselves.

In 1978 the DHSS review of the supplementary benefits system, *Social Assistance,* rejected the possibility of substantially relaxing the earnings rule for unemployed men, on the argument that part-time working by unemployed men is rare (paras. 8.18 — 24). This seems an odd argument, for if it is rare then it will not cost the DHSS and the taxpayer much to relax the rule, for few will take advantage of it. It is also odd because it does not consider the possibility that paid economic activity of any kind by unemployed men may be a good thing and should be actively encouraged. Certainly it does not seem to be in the spirit of the Beveridge Report of 1942 which is the historic basis of our social security system. Beveridge wrote (pp. 6—7):

> The State in organising security should not stifle incentive, opportunity, responsibility; in establishing a national minimum, it should leave room and encouragement for voluntary action by each individual to provide more than the minimum for himself and his family.

The letter of our social security system could not have departed further from the intended spirit.

Nosey parkers

If the unemployed are encouraged by the earnings rule not to declare part-time earnings to the authorities, they are also in the invidious position of being more likely to be caught than employed people who do not declare part of their earnings to the taxman. Those unemployed who are trying to earn a little more for themselves and their family spend considerably more time looking anxiously over their shoulders than do their employed compatriots in the black economy. Even those who engage in voluntary work have to be careful. Why is this?

If your neighbour is employed as a painter and decorator and walks out of the house on a Monday morning in white overalls with brush and pot in hand, you do not think twice about it. You do not wonder whether he's getting paid cash for this particular job, whether he's declaring it to the taxman.

If your neighbour is unemployed and walks out similarly clad, you think to yourself, 'Ay, aye, he's earning a little bit on the side.' Unemployed members of the black economy are so much more visible. You may then say, 'Good for you, lad!' But if you are bearing a grudge against either the unemployed in general or him in particular, you may decide to make an anonymous phone call to the local DHSS office. We have already seen how censorious the public can be about those fiddling the social security, and how accepting, even encouraging, toward those who decide to get one over the common enemy, the taxman.

Fred, whom we have met a couple of times already, found himself in just this situation. One week he went out each day to paint his mum's house, for free. A neighbour shopped him 'to the social' (after all, he's left-wing, supports the rights of the unemployed and is surely seen as a troublemaker by some). The investigating officer asked Fred what he'd been doing that week, and off he went round to interview Fred's mum to check the story and check that no money had changed hands.

Just as local social security offices vary enormously in their acceptance or persecution of voluntary work on the dole, so do public attitudes. Budding young athletes who have no sponsorship and can get the time to train only by becoming unemployed may actually receive public acclaim. One local rag, not exactly noted for any subversive or anarchist tendencies, hailed the arrival of one particular entrant to the dole queue in a front page article with banner headline, 'WATCH OUT, THE WORLD!':

> Brilliant local gymnast Trevor Lyons will find out if three years of sacrifice and dedication have been worthwhile when he competes in the British Olympic trials next month.
>
> Trevor has been living off supplementary benefit and the generosity of his parents since giving up his job two years ago.
>
> Now he is determined to get a deserved reward for his efforts by making the team for this year's games in Los Angeles . . . 'I may be unemployed but I am not walking the streets. I am doing what I want to. Right now I would love to get to Los Angeles,' he said.

If Trevor had been working hard at virtually any other occupation while on the dole, he would more likely have been condemned as a scrounger. Hardly anyone else is allowed to do 'as he wants' on the dole! Trevor is certainly an exception. I am sure that were the DHSS implicitly to sponsor a world beater, it would be politically embarrassing for them to receive the acclaim that Nottingham Council received for sponsoring ice dance champions Torvill and Dean. Tacit support by the DHSS for informal work has to be discreet if public uproar is not to be provoked.

In fact, the DHSS was recently instructed by the government to expand the activities of its special investigation officers and more were appointed. The public may fondly imagine these officers are doing a great job, but the absurdity of this kind of activity is highlighted by a minor incident on the outskirts of Liverpool. Joe is virtually the only black lad in an overwhelmingly white community, and after signing on one day he walked over the road, as he often does, to the parish church where he began to help the sexton tidy up the churchyard, having nothing better to do. Within minutes there was a knock at the door of the church office. A social security clerk had seen him walk over the road and start work, and asked, 'Is the lad who's just come over from the social security office helping you in the churchyard?' The church secretary, not knowing who he was, eagerly replied,

'Yes, would you like to help too?!' The clerk's reply is not recorded.

Scouse wit aside, Joe is getting a bit of a chip on his shoulder about this kind of thing. Being one of the few blacks, everyone knows him and knows he is unemployed. There is nothing he can do, legitimate or illegitimate, fearing someone is suspecting him of being on the fiddle.

Hard to plan

After lack of money, the next biggest impediment to an active life on the dole is that it is difficult to plan — to plan your money, your life, and how you and your family can best share out the work in the four economies.

When you become unemployed, you do not know whether you will be out of paid work for ten days or ten years. If it's to be ten years, you may be wise to take a holiday now while you can afford it. But if the chances of getting a job are better, you would be well advised to look for work straightaway, while you still have the contacts, the phone and the car.

But how can you tell? You can't. At first, many assume that they won't be out of paid work for long, and act accordingly. As the months go by, they begin to realize their assumption was wrong, but by then they have already committed themselves to courses of action which they are now paying for: perhaps the most common is hanging on to savings which after twelve months disqualify them from supplementary benefit.

Certainly none of us is God, who knows all things. No one knows for certain that he will not be run over by a bus tomorrow. But for an ordinary, active life, it is important that we can take for granted a certain order to everyday life. We buy our child a school uniform, on the assumption that he won't be run over tomorrow. We plan a holiday a few months ahead, assuming we'll still have a job then and can afford it. We buy a house, assuming the firm won't transfer us to the other side of the country within a month. These assumptions may turn out to be wrong, but we have to make them if we are to live.

I have an aunt who was on the waiting list for a major operation; she was told she could be called in any day with no more than a few hours' notice. This went on for eighteen months, and insidiously undermined everyday life: was it worth buying a theatre ticket for next week, let alone planning to see relatives next month, or a holiday next summer? This is exactly the position of the vast majority of the unemployed who are still hoping and looking for a paid job. How can they be nominated for a more responsible position on the committee of some voluntary organization, when no one knows whether they will continue to have the time for it if they get a paid job? How can an unemployed local councillor accept an invitation to chair a committee, rather than be just an ordinary member of it, when he would have to give it up were he to get a paid job? Is it worth paying a year's fee and joining several evening classes as a way of passing the time or improving yourself? Is it worth getting an allotment? Is it worth your wife giving up her part-time job, which may be wise if you are to be on supplementary benefit for a long time, but silly if you get a job next week since she may not be able to get another?

Decisions about money are particularly difficult. Managing on the dole requires careful budgeting, but how can you make the calculations necessary to budget when the financial future is so uncertain? It is particularly difficult to know what to do with redundancy payments. One often hears scathing comments about how the working class do not know how to handle windfalls, and those made redundant are often criticized for having 'blown it all'. But consider. You are given £5,000 redundancy money. Should you end up self-employed, you are very wise to hang on to it all. But if, as is not unlikely, you are still out of work and looking for a job in twelve months' time, you will be wise to have dispensed of £2,000 of it if you are to be eligible for supplementary benefit. A holiday of a lifetime, and the rest put into improving the house would be one rational course; you may not be able to afford either again. But say you are offered a job elsewhere and have to sell the house, and you are moving from a declining industrial area, money spent on the house may not be recouped as house prices plummet. If you are well-informed about all these possibilities, it is difficult enough to make a rational decision; but if you have been made redundant for the first time, it is unlikely you will be aware of the financial implications of social security regulations, and you may wrongly estimate your chances of getting another paid job.

Where there is mass redundancy, as at the British Steel Corporation Port Talbot works in 1980, things may be better. All the workers left together and, finding themselves in the same boat, were able to discuss their situation with each other. Building societies and banks set up portacabins on housing estates to provide advice, and BSC gave all redundant workers financial counselling. Some of the older men knew they'd never find paid work again, and could plan their finances till they received their pension at a known date in the future. But this is not typical. Usually people become unemployed here and there, and are isolated from both formal and informal sources of support and sound advice.

The unpredictability of living in the unemployed state is partly due to various social security rules, which could easily be changed. Some of it, however, is due to unemployment itself, and the simple uncertainty of not knowing if or when paid work will be offered again.

However, it cannot be stated too strongly that it is unemployment, *not the lack of paid work,* that is the cause of the problem. Those without paid work who are not unemployed do not typically suffer the same degree of uncertainty. The woman who leaves paid work in order to have a baby plans her future often with glee and may be very positive about her new life; similarly, the person who leaves paid work for further education. And some pensioners may be very positive about their retirement, though many others suffer from uncertainty and worries about both finances and health.

Two psychologists from Sheffield, Stephen McKenna and David Fryer, have done some interesting research comparing a group of redundant workers with a group of laid-off ones.

Making some workers redundant, and laying sections of the workforce off for specified periods, are both ways in which a business can shed labour. The psychological effects of the two methods on the workers themselves are dramatically different. The redundant workers displayed all the problems typical of the unemployed: financial worries, depression, impaired health and impaired general well-being. The laid-off workers' health and well-being improved. Why?

They were laid off for seven weeks, came back for one week, and then were officially on holiday for three, though most of them took the whole eleven off. Almost all of them treated the time as a sabbatical of known duration; it was possible to structure the time because it had a known end, and it was possible to use funds rationally because they knew that they would be back to their normal wages after the eleven weeks. Many of them spent the time renovating their homes, tinkering with cars and doing all the things that you put off for a rainy day but that actually require a rainy month.

McKenna and Fryer's research confirms everyday observation of mothers, students and pensioners. The experience of the unemployed of feeling rudderless and at sea, and their difficulties in structuring their days, do not derive from not having a paid job, but from the peculiar uncertainties of being *unemployed.*

These problems can also affect those who anticipate becoming unemployed. A friend in his fifties, who had only recently moved from engineering to become a university lecturer, became anxious when the cuts of the late 1970s were first announced. His position was unclear, he feared that he would lose his job on the 'last in, first out' principle, and he had a wife and family to support. He spent two very worried years as the politicking of university professors and administrators wore on interminably. Eventually it was confirmed that he would get early retirement at a specified date, with a specified golden handshake, and at last his family could begin to plan their lives again, rather than drift anxiously on from day to day. Though this man has a Christian faith, that did not make the day-to-day running of the family finances any easier, nor make it any easier to make rational decisions.

Explanations of idleness

Given the five pressures to passivity described in this chapter — lack of money, the availability and earnings rules, nosey parkers and the difficulty of planning — is it any wonder that so many of the unemployed report boredom and depression among their main problems? Is it any wonder that the unemployed, far from embodying the stereotype of busily fiddling a good living, can easily become listless, resigned and passive?

There are two more common explanations for the passivity of the unemployed. One is that they are the left-behinds. Those with the get-up-and-go have already got up and got a job. The unemployed are the inadequates, content to live dependent on the state. The evidence of this chapter strongly suggests that this explanation is unlikely to be correct. The massive pressures described afflict *all* the unemployed who are drawing social security and have not given up hope of a job. Indeed, far from the unemployed being congenitally dependent, would it not take a remarkably resilient person to carve out an active existence under such conditions?

Such perhaps is the surely incorrect explanation preferred by the successful stockbroker reading the *Daily Telegraph* on the 8.13 to Waterloo. A more academic, but also deficient explanation, is that preferred by Marie Jahoda, co-author of the classic 1930s study of the unemployed in the Austrian town of Marienthal and mentor of many counsellors of the unemployed.

She argues that, in addition to the manifest function of a wage, paid work also provides five latent functions for the worker: a time structure; enlargement of the scope of social experience into less emotionally charged, and in some ways simpler, areas than family life; participation in a collective purpose or effort; the receipt of status and identity; and required regular activity. These things structure life and provide goals,

99

and their loss causes the purposelessness, structurelessness and drifting of life on the dole.

Jahoda is surely right that people need goals and a purpose to their lives, but who says that only a paid job can provide these? Surely this is to elevate paid work to a position that idolizes work beyond all reasonable bounds? As Ray Pahl has retorted, many working-class people find more purpose and fulfilment in their allotment, pigeon-keeping or playing in the local brass band than they do at work. It is precisely Jahoda's 'latent functions' — rigid time structure, domination of the week by the paid job, the requirement to turn up at work at a specified time, and so on — that form the industrial work discipline that people have such mixed feelings about (chapter 2). Some people are all too glad on retirement or motherhood to lose these things.

The fact surely is that human beings are able to choose from a whole range of purposes and activities by which they can structure their lives. Paid work is an important one, and for many it has become so important that its unasked-for loss causes suffering of the form Jahoda describes. Her theory explains their experience adequately, but it fails to explain the experience of many of those who leave paid work for positive reasons such as motherhood or education; it fails to explain the experience of those few unemployed who do make a decent life while unemployed; and it fails to explain the not insignificant minority whose physical health and psychological well-being remains unchanged or improves on unemployment. It lets society off the hook for the way it treats the unemployed, for it portrays their pains as inevitable; and it tells the unemployed that their only hope of psychological well-being is to go and get a paid job.

Jahoda's theory is ultimately deficient because it takes the contented wage slave as some kind of norm. Human beings are much more flexible than that, and able to invent other ways of living than to devote themselves to the idol of paid work. After all, just over 50 per cent of the British people neither have, nor want, paid work. Why should the other 50 per cent be made into some kind of norm?

Fryer's researches suggest that Jahoda's theory is incomplete. She is surely correct that many of the unemployed miss the structure and purpose provided by paid work and that many are depressed and passive. But what evidence is there that the one is the sole or even main cause of the other? We have already observed that *anyone* put into a position of low income, with regulations that ban or inhibit most forms of creative or purposeful activity, and complete uncertainty as to both short- and long-term future, is likely to become depressed and passive. You would not need to have lost your job to feel down in such a situation. Also we have noted that many of those without the benefits of paid work and its latent functions are by no means passive and depressed; namely, many mothers, mature students and pensioners, not to mention those temporarily laid-off.

It would seem that people are sentenced to idleness not by the loss of a paid job *per se,* but by the lack of a good income, restrictive regulations, and the lack of any alternative purpose. I aim to show in Part Three that those few who are able to make a decent life on the dole are those who have somehow or other got around these lacks. I will argue that our society could choose to ensure that these three lacks do not automatically accompany unemployment.

If Marie Jahoda is correct, then all we can do as a society is to try to create more full-time paid jobs. If the critique of her view is correct, then in addition to creating more paid jobs there is also much more we can do as a society: we can change the circumstances in which people become unemployed so that they are reprieved from the sentence to idleness and can once again become active, contributing members of the community, whether or not they find paid work.

6   Sentenced to Idleness (2)

In chapter 5 I described five pressures that help push the unemployed into passivity, a kind of cold-storage existence. I argued that this passivity is not an inevitable reaction to the loss of paid work so much as a likely response to the treatment dealt by our society to the unemployed. Before we can proceed in Part Three to look at some ways in which some unemployed people have rejected this sentence to idleness, we must understand that, though all the unemployed are subject to the five pressures, most of the unemployed are also subject to some other pressures to passivity. These do not derive directly from being unemployed, but they afflict many of the unemployed in a peculiarly powerful and painful way.

Woman's work, man's work

The one group of unemployed people that society does expect to be active are married women. It is generally felt that 'they're all right, because they can always go back to being housewives'. In her book *Redundant Women,* Angela Coyle found that the women she studied who were made redundant by the closure of a clothing factory in Harrogate did not feel at all happy with this role they were expected to slot easily back into. After all, many of them had paid jobs for exactly the same reasons as men: for the money, the company, and for getting out of the intense atmosphere of the home.

Just as there is a blanket assumption that women will easily slot back into work in the home, so there is a blanket assumption that men do not have this capability. Home is a woman's place, and housework is woman's work. Men need paid work outside the home if they are to be real men. That is the unspoken assumption of all those who claim unemployment to be a natural disaster for a man but entry to a different form of work for a woman.

Unfortunately, the assumption about men can be all too accurate. Certainly there are some men who see unemployment as a chance to become more involved with their families, a few of whom will appear in Part Three, but what research has been done into the household roles of unemployed men in the present recession gives no hope whatsoever of a mass reversal of roles. Few indeed are the number of unemployed men who want to take the children off to school while their wives go out and earn the family's bread.

Research indicates that unemployment is unlikely to change radically the respective roles played by husband and wife. More often, it accentuates whatever relationship was there already.

In a classic study, *Family and Social Network* (Tavistock 1957), Elizabeth Bott identified two kinds of family. There are those where the couple do household tasks and leisure activities together, and they are relatively independent of friends, relatives and neighbours. (Incidentally, such people may find it fairly easy to move to a new job.) Then there are those where husband and wife live much more segregated lives: the man finds companionship down at pub or club, and the woman is more likely to turn to neighbours or mother than to husband for help with looking after the children. Such spouses are as deeply embedded in a social life outside the home as in the marriage itself.

When the man becomes unemployed, there is the possibility in 'joint' families of him deciding to expand his participation in the household economy, with the result that the marriage becomes even more of a working partnership. But in 'segregated' families, this is not really an option. She really does not want him in the house all day getting in her way; she is so used to setting the standards of housework in the home that she does not welcome an intruder into her personal domain. He for his part feels much more at home spending the day outside in the informal economy, doing odd jobs for mates and socializing with them.

Lorna McKee and Colin Bell, in a recent research study of marital relations in times of unemployment, found that the social life of wife as well as husband can be curtailed by his unemployment. Having been used to running her own day, the wife may find her unemployed husband controlling her social life, 'allowing' her to go out or not, and her female friends may stop coming to visit when he is around in the home. The presence of one man may wreck the normal social life of women. It is not surprising, then, that some wives struggling to keep house on supplementary benefit may resign themselves to further scrimp and save in order to release spare cash to get him out of the house and down to the local.

In some regions, there is a powerful tradition that men do not do housework, and that roles in the home should be segregated. Lydia Morris studied forty redundant steelworkers from Port Talbot and did not find a single case of real role reversal. The man who did *most* housework still left most of it to his wife after her return at 2 p.m. from her paid morning job, and in any case she was dissatisfied with the standard of what work he had done. It was she who prepared the children's tea before going back to work again at 5 p.m. He would not clean the windows, as this would be visible to the general public. The husband who claimed to spend most time looking after the children actually took them in his car to his mother. Women in this sample who needed someone to look after their children would be far more likely to ask nan or a neighbour than their unemployed husband.

Men of working age often do seem to find their male image tarnished if they are seen to be too involved in child care. One community worker told me that the children's work in his community centre is greatly aided by voluntary help, but with one exception this is female. This is even though the centre is located in an estate where there are a lot of unemployed men. The one exception, significantly, defines himself as retired. He is about sixty, and was made redundant after thirty-five years with the same firm. He was very angry about this, but has now found a role for himself helping out at the centre. He is able to do this because he feels he has completed his working life; he has made his contribution as a man, so it is no longer unmanly for him to get involved in work with children. I have certainly observed that some men who were pretty distant dads can feel much more free to play the part of grandad when the time comes.

So there are many families where the man is unemployed — reporting boredom as a main problem of being unemployed — and with a wife who has a paid job, perhaps full time, *and* who does all the housework. The most the husband may do is to transport the kids to nan's. Surely the problem in such families, plagued simultaneously by both overwork and boredom, is not the *lack* of work, but the unjust and absurd *distribution* of work within the home. Deeply held traditions about the roles for man and woman are a major problem, sentencing the man to idleness.

However, this picture of families with a wife with two jobs (one in the formal economy and one in the household economy) and a husband with none is true for less than a third of families with an unemployed husband. This is because wives with unemployed husbands are less likely to have a paid job than wives with employed husbands. The most recent *General Household Survey* (1982) found that, whereas 59 per cent of employed husbands have a working wife, only 29 per cent of unemployed husbands have a wife who works outside the home.

There are several possible reasons for this dramatic difference, and research has yet to establish which are the most important. One we have already referred to: if the husband receives supplementary benefit, the family will not improve their financial situation by the wife working unless her wage comes to more than the amount of supplementary benefit. Her working may well be worthwhile if the man is on unemployment benefit which is being topped up with supplementary benefit and she has a full-time paid job. But where the family is no longer entitled to unemployment benefit, and especially if the woman's paid work is part time, then — by the time travelling and other expenses of going to work are counted — the family may actually lose money by her going out to work.

A second reason for women giving up their paid jobs when their husbands become unemployed is that either or both of them do not like the idea of her being the breadwinner. They feel it is not right.

A third reason is that the woman in a 'joint' family may feel that if she gave up work, then the couple can enjoy more time together, in the way that some women give up paid work when their husband retires so that they can enjoy retirement together. However, Dennis Marsden's research found that even with these couples, the husband tends not to take on jobs in the house usually done by the wife. In fact, there is a tendency for wives to put in even more than usual commitment into their household tasks and enlarge them, with the result that there is little left for the man to do at home. With reduced income, shopping involves hunting for bargains, cooking involves less pre-prepared food, washing may have to be done by hand, all of which takes more time. If these tasks are not taken on by the husband, and they rarely are, his unemployment simply means more work for her.

There are two further possible reasons for the correlation between unemployment for the husband and working in the home for the wife. One is that, since unemployment is concentrated in particular regions, it is possible that husband and wife may both happen to be unemployed, independent of their financial or emotional relationship to each other. This seems unlikely on the surface, because most of the 'at home' wives of unemployed husbands report themselves not as unemployed but as having withdrawn from the labour market. However, this should not be taken at face value since married women are discouraged from registering as unemployed.

The other possibility is that unemployed men with working wives may have opportunities to find paid work through their wives' contacts at work and through the generally enlarged social circle that their wives' paid employment often brings.

More sophisticated research exploring the stages at which women move in and out of paid employment in relation to their husband's unemployment will have to be done before these last two explanations can be properly assessed, but it does seem likely from what unemployed families say that the first three explanations — that wives give up their paid job for financial and emotional reasons resulting from their husband's unemployment — are very important.

Whatever the reasons, it seems that the chances are high that the wife will end up at home without a paid job and the pressure will be on the husband to go and get a job. This does not make for the happiness of either, if she would prefer to be out of the house working some of the time, and if he feels surplus to requirements in the family nest.

It seems clear to me that if all men were freed to consider the possibility of being homemakers and were given the right by society not to work if they so chose; and if all women were freed to have as much right to a paid job as men, then the problem of unemployment would be very largely solved. This is *not* to say that unemployed men should be *forced* into being houseworkers, for that is precisely the problem that many unemployed women face now, namely, being *expected* to return happily to the kitchen sink. No, it is a matter of people being freed to consider options. The problem is surely as much one of rigid sexual stereotypes as of a crisis in the formal economy.

I am not saying that such expectations can, or should, be changed overnight. In particular, 'segregated' families, whose stability and happiness depends on the needs and demands of each spouse being met by a range of people outside the nuclear family, may be destroyed by the spouses attempting a joint working relationship. Community life may well suffer too, for it is often members of precisely such families that are the mainstay of the pub, the women's institute, the darts team, the playgroup, the church and all the other little groups that keep community life thriving. In such families, it is essential that resources be found to enable the unemployed husband to find activities in the informal economy outside of the home.

Making do

It is sometimes assumed that unemployment cannot be as bad in the 1980s, cushioned by 'generous' welfare payments, as it was in the harsh 1930s. However, a big change has occurred since then that greatly reduces the value of welfare benefits.

When a nation first industrializes and economic growth begins to occur, the growth is usually fuelled by the consumer demands of the upper and middle classes. Such was the case in Britain in the nineteenth century and to a large extent up to the Second World War. While the Edwardian upper classes and their swinging successors in the 1920s were demanding ever more in the way of posh clothes and luxury motor cars, and while the middle-class suburban dream was fuelling the demand for owner-occupied houses and a nice little Austin, not to mention new ring roads and suburban railways, the majority of the working class felt much as they always had done: poor, and not a part of this affluent society. Theirs was a culture of poverty, of resourcefulness, frugality, self-sufficiency and the willingness to share.

However, there came a time when all the middle classes had got a nice little car and a nice little house and all the things they needed to put in it. If the idol of economic growth was to be assuaged, then there had to develop a similar demand from the working class. For this, the old working class culture of frugality and self-sufficiency had to be destroyed. According to Jeremy Seabrook, this is precisely the story of the consumer society since the 1950s. What we British lament in our nostalgia for the sharing and commitment to each other that flourished in the Second World War was in fact the last flowering of the traditional working-class culture of sharing in adversity. The washing machine and the Ford Anglia, boons though they were, destroyed that for ever.

This means that, whereas somehow you scraped by in the 1930s on a pittance of national assistance, now it is often a losing battle to make do on what is objectively a much bigger sum of social security. Seabrook sums it all up in the words of one old lady from Sheffield: 'Working class people used to be proud of how much they could do with very little money; now people feel ashamed of how little they can do without a lot of it.' Rather than gaining pride from busying yourself to keep your family fed and clothed, there is now demoralization at what you have not got. Demoralization and an active life do not go together.

There are some groups which do have pride in making do on little, and some of them seem to get by all right on social security. Anyone in the ecology movement who believes passionately in conservation takes a pride in using as few material resources as possible to lead a civilized life. Some of them positively relish avoiding the cash economy; as much as possible they spin their own wool, make their clothes, grow their food, and use wind power to generate their own electricity. Some immigrants still share a vibrant extended family and community life, sharing with each other what little they have in the face of being excluded from the white community. I remember one middle-class voluntary worker in Bath telling me how humbled she feels by her friendship with three West Indian single mothers on social security, living in the flats where the city council dumps its problem families. Living hand to mouth, whenever one of these girls has a windfall such as a present from a distant relative or a back-dated cheque from the social security, she would immediately share it with the other two and their children. My friend had never seen sharing like this in her middle-class church just up the road. The widow's mite indeed, alive and well in Bath!

But conservation and immigrant cultures are miles away from the working-class culture in which most of Britain's unemployed find themselves today. Indeed, the sharing and making-do on less that ecologists and some blacks treasure is despised by many a working class family, perhaps because it reminds them of the poverty they may have escaped from only recently. For most of the unemployed, it is very painful to have been invited to the feast of the consumer society, and then have

109

the door slammed in your face because you have lost your ticket — a paid job in the formal economy. For many, unemployment means sitting dejected on the doormat, watching through the window at the feast going on inside.

Demoralization

There are a few housing schemes where the trust that makes ordinary life possible has either broken down or never become established. Driving through such estates, you may notice that none of the gardens are tended. This is not necessarily because people do not care, but because anything planted will be vandalized overnight. A few experiences of this kind are enough to put off any would-be gardener, or indeed anyone who'd just like things to be nice and tidy outside the house. Replacing broken windows can also be a soul-destroying task if they are to be smashed again within days.

This kind of experience can be demoralizing for anyone, not just the unemployed, living on such an estate. But it can be particularly difficult for the unemployed, and such estates usually have more than the normal quota of unemployed. Those with jobs in the formal economy are able to escape during their hours of paid work to a workplace where there is trust and co-operation, and they may have money enough to escape with their families during leisure hours. The unemployed, though, are trapped, not least because such estates are often on the outskirts of large cities and it can be expensive getting a bus out. Any productive activity that they may be able to manage in the black, informal or household economy has to be within the estate and is vulnerable to vandalism. Using redundancy money to do up your house may be money and time and your own labour down the drain. It is less disheartening to stay in and watch the telly.

In such non-communities there is often not the trust or the faith for people easily to co-operate and form community organizations, even though it is precisely on these estates that there is most need for voluntary work in the community:

whether it be looking after and reassuring the frightened elderly, running errands for mums with sick kids who cannot leave them in order to walk a mile to phone for a doctor (nearer phones having been vandalized), physically tidying up the neighbourhood, or lobbying the local council. There are marvellous exceptions, such as Glasgow's Easterhouse and Edinburgh's Craigmillar estates where community organizations have flourished in recent years, putting on art and music festivals and starting local businesses as well as more traditional voluntary work, dramatically raising the confidence in the estate of both residents and city councillors.

But without such organizations, what can the unemployed family do? Even if they have a tent or hospitable relatives and could go for a cheap holiday, no one in their right mind goes on holiday from their area without insuring the contents of their house, and the unemployed cannot afford the hiked-up premiums charged for households with their kind of address. The employed may with luck be able to laugh at getting yet another new telly and video on the insurance when their house is emptied for the fifth time, but that is no joke for the uninsured unemployed.

Getting paid work may also be more difficult. You are less likely to be offered a job when the employer notices your address. Banks are less likely to provide a loan should you contemplate going self-employed, and who would consider investing in equipment that will be so vulnerable? You only have to see the shopping parades where one shop after another is empty and boarded up, with the vandalized telephone kiosks outside, to understand why people don't resolve their unemployment by going self-employed in such an area.

If other people in such estates are not prepared to invest money in their homes and cars and gardens, then you will not find a demand for odd little jobs. You are not going to be able to top up your dole by earning an occasional fiver digging a pensioner's garden, or erecting a greenhouse for a neighbour. Nor can you spend your time fixing your mates' cars or motor bikes for them if everyone is unemployed or moving in and out of temporary unemployment and there are no cars or bikes to fix.

In sum, in a few estates the unemployed are inhibited from activity because of the lack of opportunity and the possible destruction of the fruits of any labour. To add injury to insult, the cost of living may be higher. Not only insuring, replacing or mending your vandalized possessions, but also the price of food and other basics: either you shop locally in the one or two shops still surviving which are invariably expensive and poorly stocked, or you get the bus to somewhere else. To pay £3 for a taxi to take your weekly shopping home from a hypermarket some miles away may well be the cheapest way of shopping. That's one expense the DHSS do not budget for when they work out social security rates. It has to come from somewhere else in the family budget.

The dependent British?

I have no hard evidence, but I sometimes wonder whether we British tend to produce rather dependent personalities. Compared to American schools, where the child is encouraged to interrupt the teacher and ask questions and where the desired product is a free citizen able to stand on his or her own feet, is not the aim of our schools much more to teach the child to 'know its place'? Unasked-for questions, still more suggestions, from the classroom floor are often defined by the teacher as 'cheek', and the natural curiosity of the child is suppressed; I know several American children in British schools who have found this out to their cost. Knowledge is something possessed by the teacher, and is imparted to the child from above. This prepares the child for a class society in which 'they', those who run things, are the ones who 'know', and woe betide the ordinary mortal if he or she should suggest otherwise.

I am not idolizing the American way of life. Though it is refreshing to find there a people who feel they are masters and mistresses of their own fate, many of them may well be deluding themselves. There are very real constraints on the freedom of the poor American to better him or herself, but failure to do so is likely to be experienced as personal failure rather than simply one's allotted place in the social order. However, it does seem to me that the British are peculiarly pessimistic about the possibility of taking charge of their own lives; sometimes this is simple realism about the class system into which we are born, but at other times this defeatism can really limit our horizons. Put simply, if Americans are prone to imagining they can fix things when in fact they cannot, we British are prone to imagining there is nothing we can do when in fact there is.

When the system fails you in Britain, as it does if you become unemployed, then it is seen as 'their' job to provide. What autonomy the unemployed once had to control their own lives has been taken away. Time was when if you were a bit short and couldn't manage the rent one week because you'd just paid the electricity bill, the rent collector would quietly mark up the book as paid but actually give you a week's credit. Other creditors could do similar favours, so it became possible for the poor family to manage the ebb and flow of money coming in and out of the house, just as it is in a middle-class family or in a business with overdraft facilities. But for those on supplementary benefit today, the rent is deducted at source from your benefit, so that the control of this ebb and flow is taken from your hands. For the best of paternalist reasons — the protection of a few families from a husband who drinks or gambles away all the social security or from a wife who is a 'bad manager' — the system takes away from the unemployed yet one more area of personal control of their finances. The old pawn shops are being replaced by loan sharks, and if you do not repay on time, they go to the magistrates, who will almost certainly order that £5 per week is deducted direct from your social security at source. Again, you are blamed for your financial difficulties, cannot be trusted to sort it out yourself and the 'Nanny State' will have to do it for you. Note that Nanny has not herself tried to bring up a family of two on supplementary benefit of £60 a week.

With the public expenditure cuts of the late 1970s and early 1980s, a massive waiting list for council house repairs has developed in many cities. Many of the families living in this accommodation are unemployed. Many are quite competent to do the repairs themselves, and if they were allowed so to do and reimbursed any expenses, then that would help solve the problem of council house repairs *and* provide satisfying activity for the unemployed person. The chairman of one housing authority gave me some quite convincing bureaucratic, economic and political reasons for not letting people do their own repairs (like they have already paid for this in their rent, so they would be doing something themselves that they have already paid someone else to do), but the fact remains that the unemployed are left at home seeing a job needing doing that they are not allowed to do.

Owner occupiers who have redundancy money frequently use some of it to do up their own home, using their own labour. Council tenants are much more limited in what they can do, and most of the unemployed are council tenants (58 per cent, compared with 34 per cent of the general population). Of those who have been unemployed for more than two years, four out of five are council tenants and are reduced to impotency as far as major household repairs are concerned.

Anger

So long as society blames the unemployed for their own unemployment, some of the unemployed will take this attitude to heart and blame themselves. They will turn on themselves their natural anger at having been made useless; the resentment will go inward, they will feel themselves to be failures and become depressed. It won't be easy for anyone feeling like that to take charge of their lives and start living the best they can in the circumstances.

Whether this vicious cycle begins depends very much on how much anger is felt on becoming unemployed, and whether it is easily expressed.

Some people feel very angry at being made redundant or at being fired, because it is sometimes the best workers who get the sack. Many firms, particularly in Britain, want a placid workforce who will do as they are told, whether or not it is the best way of getting the job done (not unlike many schools who want pupils who speak only when spoken to by teacher). Because we still live in a class society in which people become managers not through merit alone but also through inherited advantage, and in which some quite talented people are stuck in basic grades, it is not uncommon to find a manager who personally feels insecure with a workforce that may include experienced people with bright ideas as to how the job could be done better. Such a manager can easily respond by stifling initiative, and it is not unusual for the manager to secure his position simply by getting rid of the brighter employee. This can be done on the basis that 'he/she doesn't fit in very well', which indeed may be the case if there is antagonism from other workers who feel threatened by a colleague with initiative. The fired person can feel very bitter about this.

Not only do the best workers sometimes get fired first, so also do some of the better firms get closed down. The Harrogate factory studied by Coyle had only recently benefited from a time-and-motion study, productivity was high, and it was profitable. It was closed because of a plan of rationalization on a nation-wide (sometimes it is global) scale. When a workforce has been putting in extra effort and is making a plant profitable as a result, and then the plant gets closed down for completely different reasons, the disillusion and anger can be considerable.

So the unemployed person may be more or less angry. They may also be more or less able to express it and get it out of their system constructively. Where there is mass redundancy, it is both obvious to the worker that it is not his or her own individual fault, and there are others around in the same boat who may provide a ready ear for any grievance. The ease with which the unemployed person can express his or her anger may also be eased or hindered by the attitude of the family. Redundant

115

formal economy, jobs that the formal labour market would deem uneconomic, and remarkably similar to the black economy in terms of tasks done, for whom, for what wages, and under what conditions of security. Trade unions object to some MSC schemes on the grounds that they are taking work from the formal economy; often, however, they are taking work from the black and informal economies, so that the state is coming to control yet another one of the areas where ordinary people once had some freedom. A major voluntary social service agency in Sheffield has objected for precisely this reason to what it sees as an MSC takeover of voluntary work.

The activities of the unemployed are tightly controlled, and may become more so. Is it that we believe three million of our fellow human beings and their families do not want to live active, purposeful lives, adding to the real wealth of themselves and their communities? What on earth do we think they may get up to that will detract from the true wealth of the community? Why do we not trust them?

The unemployed are sentenced to passivity. How may they be freed for activity?

PART THREE

Hope on the Dole

7   How to Free the Unemployed

The Right likes to believe the inactivity of the unemployed is due to their laziness. The Left likes to believe it is due to their lack of paid work. In the previous two chapters I have argued that neither is necessary to explain the passive life of the unemployed. It is explicable in terms of the peculiar position our society puts the unemployed in.

According to the Right, there is little society can do directly for the unemployed other than offer them ill-paid MSC schemes. According to the Left, there is little to be done other than provide more paid jobs, and if their economic analysis is correct there is little hope of that happening till some years after the next election that they succeed in winning; in other words, there is no hope for the unemployed in Britain till at best the early 1990s.

But if the wasting away of the unemployed is due largely to how society in general, and the state in particular, treats them, then there is much that can be done to free them to a productive life in the non-formal economies, alongside efforts to increase or share employment in the formal economy.

Not only do we diminish ourselves as a community by unnecessarily condemning the unemployed to waste away on our behalf, we also lose out from the loss of their productive efforts in the non-formal economies.

If a man will not work . . .

Many, including many economists, will doubtless object to the thrust of this book. For them, an unemployed person — whatever he is doing or not doing — is a drain on the wealth creators, that is on those with paid jobs in the formal economy who have to pay taxes to support the unemployed. They may feel that my glib talk about the unemployed adding to the wealth of the

121

community is all very fine for the unemployed, but the taxpayer still knows that his wealth is being diminished by the taxes he has to pay to support these fortunates amusing themselves at his expense.

This really is a fatuous objection. Can the true wealth of the community really be measured only by goods and services that happen to be paid for? Is turning raw meat into an appetising dish adding to the community's wealth if done in a restaurant or works canteen, but not if done at home or at an old folks' luncheon club? Surely this is rubbish. It is, of course, largely the labour of women that is not counted as real work, nor the product as real wealth, and the labour of those in the black economy that the state cannot control is likewise not counted as creating wealth.

Certainly an unemployed woman cooking a meal at home is not adding to the wealth of *the government* in the way that a chef paying taxes is. Certainly there is a transfer of cash from the taxpaying chef to the unemployed woman. But to say that one is adding to the wealth of the community, whereas the other is a drain on it, is manifest nonsense.

The objection is sometimes put another way. If a man will not work, then let him not eat. Certainly a society should not have to carry parasites of able body and mind, and as a statement of fact it is true that if a person ceases work in all four economies then he will starve, unless someone else (usually a wife) decides to look after him.

However, the 'if a man will not work, let him not eat' objection is really very hypocritical. If we want people to work, then why on earth do we discourage work by the unemployed in the non-formal economies when there is not enough work to go around in the formal economy? Why do we so often think only of paid work in the formal economy as work? After all, when St Paul wrote his famous sentence, paid work was even less important in comparison to the other forms of work than it is today. Why do we think he was referring solely to paid work?

Surely the important thing is that work be done that produces a product or service that people value. Is an employee making cosmetics to the value of £50,000 per annum really creating more wealth than the amateur artist or a woman giving birth? Is a garage mechanic getting a car ready for the road doing something of more value than the parent getting its child ready for school?

The free-market theory of economics draws out of the hat a dictum that if people really want something, then they will pay for it. Well, this is an interesting idea, but it fails to account for so much. The new-born babe, the labour of the housewife, the child all scrubbed and washed are no less valued because no one pays for them. (Well, some men perhaps would value their wife's labour more if they had to pay for it, but that's another story. Certainly it will be a sad day when everything has to be paid for. Is not this where many fear the American way of life to be heading?)

Just look at your own life for a minute. Is your labour at your place of paid employment so much more important than your unpaid labour bringing up your children? Whom does your child value most — its mother or its schoolteacher? Which gets paid, which not? Is your accountant really more valuable to you than your dustman or the kid who brings you your Sunday paper, simply because you pay him a lot more? Which of these could you least do without? Who do you respect more — your vicar or your solicitor? Whom do you pay more?

Then there is the experience of those who have opted out of paid work for some vocation which they believe to be more important or more fulfilling, even though it is not paid or paid little. The commonest are those who leave paid work in order to have children. There are those who leave paid work to look after sick relatives. There are those mothers who, when their children have grown up, decide not to go back to paid work because there are more valuable things for them to be doing in the voluntary sector.

There are also younger voluntary workers. John Vincent, a Methodist minister who has set up a range of community work projects in inner city Sheffield, regularly employs young people who have become disillusioned with the real value of the work that they have been trained for: a biology graduate who really does not want to spend her life in the drug industry, a carpenter working for the local council who sees how the group norms at his place of work are destroying human values. These people spend time thinking and working and reflecting with Vincent, and discover how many really valuable jobs there are to be done in the run-down inner city that nobody is doing and yet the market will not pay for. The jobs get done on a mixture of dole and MSC funds.

Or take my own experience. I worked for four years on a research project that had been funded by the then Social Science Research Council. The SSRC committee in London had approved it as a worthy recipient of some tens of thousands of pounds of the taxpayers' money (early 1970 prices). I found the research interesting, but really it was of no great value to the community at large, nor was it pushing forward the frontiers of knowledge. Then I found myself having an extended sabbatical on the dole, and immediately I noticed that my ex-colleagues were showing far more interest in my work and writing. Having avoided the committee vetting system, at last I was doing some rather original work. Of course, neighbours and relatives who didn't read what I wrote had no way of judging its value other than the source of its funding: 'How can you possibly justify amusing yourself like that at the taxpayer's expense?' they would say. Trying to persuade them that the taxpayer previously had been paying about three times as much for work generally agreed by my peers to be inferior was an uphill task. But it destroyed for me for ever any idea I may have once had that the value of work may be measured by the amount of money paid for it, or by the source of that money.

John Vincent goes so far as to argue that not only is there little correlation between the real value of labour and its market price, but that there can actually be an inverse correlation. Jobs in high technology industries command the highest wages, but tend to produce the least necessary goods and services. Some indeed are positively damaging, such as armaments and some drugs. For the jobs we can least do without — road sweeping, cleaning, motherhood — we pay little or nothing.

This should not be, according to free-market theorists. According to them, firms are in business to make a profit, and they can do this only by selling to people goods and services that they want. The more they want something, the more they will pay. But do firms actually operate like this? Several studies, not to mention the everyday experience of most employees and managers, suggest not. John K. Galbraith has argued, in his books *The Affluent Society* and *The New Industrial State,* that firms cannot be tossed hither and thither by the whims of consumer demand. You are not going to set up a production line to produce Model T Ford cars if there is the faintest chance that the public next year will decide of its own accord that it doesn't like these new-fangled machines after all and would rather spend its surplus income dancing the Charleston at slap-up parties. If that were to be the case, then Henry Ford would have been better off going into catering. No, firms advertise in order to try to create a predictable demand. It doesn't matter how many different brands of soap powder are advertised, so long as the public are persuaded that they need soap powder. Firms after profit, then, do not just respond to people's wants as expressed through the price they are prepared to pay; demand is actively manipulated.

Galbraith takes the analysis further. Many firms are not after profit anyway. Who takes decisions within a firm? Employees at various levels (managers are employees too). What do these decision makers want at all costs? To be sure that their job is secure. Now profitability may not achieve this, for improved productivity may lead to job loss, including my own! What guarantees my job is that the firm expands: *growth* is what is really in the interest of those who make decisions within a firm.

There is debate over Galbraith's analysis, but what is not in doubt from the many studies of the past few decades of how firms actually operate is that firms do not respond directly to the expressed demands of the consumer. There really is no evidence that the things that cost the most are the things that people value most, still less that they are the things that are of most value in any more ultimate sense.

A modern St Francis?

The fact is that there are lots of really valuable jobs needing doing, and the free market fails to get them done. They are either not done, or done for nothing outside the money economy. At the same time, there are lots of unemployed who do not want to do nothing. They must be freed to do whatever they would like to do. I mean *freed,* not told. Bodies like the Social Science Research Council or the MSC are rarely as good as the individual person, family or local neighbourhood at knowing what needs doing.

Pete, you may remember, has been unemployed for many years by choice, and lives in a tower block. A bachelor in his mid-thirties, kids are always popping into his flat to play on his computer or to go exploring the odd patches of wild ground in his part of the city which he knows like the back of his hand. While I'm writing this, he's gone off with a few of them camping for a week, showing them how to survive comfortably in the wilds. Most of them have parents who cannot afford the price of a school trip or a Scout camp, but for a few pence on a discount bus ticket, Pete and the kids can get out to the countryside and live rough. It's a pound a day, all in. Pete has to pay for it out of his dole, so there is no way he's going to price the kids out of something they absolutely love. These trips are not planned in advance. If some children turn up at the flat and say they'd like to go, then Pete just asks how many of them there are and how long they want to go for, and off they go. In effect, Pete is playing the much needed role of uncle. He adamantly maintains that he doesn't want kids of his own, for he is far too free-floating an individual for that. But he intuitively understands how much kids value adults other than parents who are genuinely interested in them and who have worthwhile skills to impart. The kids' parents, for their part, probably trust Pete with their offspring more than they would most teachers. He has proved himself.

Pete would never call what he does 'voluntary work' or 'community work', still less 'doing good'. He's just being himself, doing what he enjoys with others who enjoy it too. A school or adventure training school that provided the same service to the community would cost it out at some hundreds of pounds a week. All Pete has is two tents (for the kids; he sleeps out usually) and his dole. Surely that is value for money? For him, for the kids, for their parents, and for society.

I don't think Pete has ever been paid for any of the odd things he does for people since he's been on the dole. A friend who has a full-time but badly paying job, and who has a very busy life, has recently moved house, and has neither time nor money to get all the redecorating done. A self-employed builder is doing the bigger jobs; a friend on the dole is doing some of it for the odd tenner; and Pete is doing the bit the others do not want to do (stripping off the old wallpaper), which took him a long weekend. He had some difficulty convincing the beneficiary that he really does not want any payment for it. It's not that he's scared of social security snoopers, he just isn't interested in money.

Clearly Pete is exceptional, but he does reveal how much of real value there is waiting to be done, and the satisfactions gained from a job well done and from the pleasure given to people by serving them. I cannot imagine that either the free market or the MSC could possibly arrange for them to be served as effectively. Certainly, when Pete takes these 'deprived' kids camping, he is fulfilling the three positive functions of work, as outlined by Schumacher: providing a necessary or useful good or service, perfecting his gifts and skills, and serving other people.

How more of the unemployed may be freed to live as Pete lives naturally is discussed in the final chapter. In the meantime, we will look at him and some others who are unemployed and doing something off their own bat, to see how they do it.

Not a life of leisure!

When I explained to John why I wanted to interview him, he began, 'Well, here I am living my life of leisure . . . except it ain't a life of leisure!' I could not agree more. No way am I arguing that what is needed for the unemployed is 'education for leisure'.

Leisure exists only as a contrast to work and when you have money. Leisure is what makes wage slavery worthwhile; and a wage is what makes leisure possible.

What the unemployed could possibly have is a working life not so dissimilar from that of the land-owning aristocrat. There is in each case an income guaranteed independent of work. Neither has earned their income. It is an accident of birth: for the one, the accident of being born into a wealthy family; for the other, of being born into a wealthy society. Neither speaks of leisure. Wealthy families trust their offspring to use their resources wisely. Our society could trust the unemployed in the same way. As with the aristocrat, there are plenty of things to do, and life could be all of a piece, without our industrial distinction between work and leisure.

The only unemployed who talk of leisure are some of those in good health who are made redundant in their late fifties or take early retirement with a golden handshake. One such group, made redundant from a steelworks in 1980, includes many who talk of enjoying a hard-earned period of leisure, with two or three holidays a year, regular golf and so on. The feeling can be, 'I'm much better off than those who have to retire at 65 because they may not have the time or the health to enjoy what I'm enjoying'. Moreover, the moral climate is supportive for leisure. Not only do they have the money to enjoy it, but also this money has been earned, they feel, by their own labour over three or four decades.

128

A strategy

Marie Jahoda is surely correct that a purpose or structure is essential for satisfactory living. However, I have argued, first, that people can get a structure and purpose from lots of things other than paid employment and, secondly, that they need not depend on that structure being provided *for* them. Human beings are able to create their own goals and structure, though they can be brainwashed into thinking otherwise. After all, that is what women — even those of low IQ and with no qualifications — do when they decide to have children and daily manage an entire household; though there may be advice in plenty, no one orders them how to do it, how to structure the housework or what standards to keep. It is nonsense to say that a paid job is essential if we are to have structures and goals. After all, mothers and aristocrats have these without a paid job.

So it would seem that to live creatively and constructively, even though society has denied you a paid job, you must:

1 Abandon any idea that a paid job is a must. In other words, you must accept the fact that you are unemployed. Then you can begin to plan and organize and take control of your life (see below).

2 Find something you want to do, and agree as a family/household to structure your affairs in an appropriate way (see chapter 8).

3 Since lack of money is a major cause of idleness among the unemployed, try to find some extra cash or resources so that your new way of life can be properly capitalized (see chapter 9).

Goodbye, wage slavery!

The unemployed are urged by well-meaning official leaflets to continue to look avidly for paid work. Leaflets assume that without the structure of a paid job the person will go to pieces, so they advise him to make job-hunting itself as much as possible like a job: with office hours, and commitment to it even though the 'job' seems rather unproductive.

This course of action is likely to lead to one of two things. If you are lucky, to a paid job. If you are unlucky, to despair and considerable delay in adjusting to unemployment.

From the material I have presented so far in this book, it seems that you are unlikely to be able to make much of a life of unemployment until you have abandoned hope of a job. By this, I don't mean that you convince yourself that you will never again get a job, but that as a day-to-day assumption you take it for granted that you won't get a job tomorrow, or next week, or next month. You are not going to spend all your time looking for a paid job that is not there, because you have better things to be doing in the meantime. Scanning the papers, keeping on the grapevine, and applying for the occasional job become one activity among several, not *the* activity around which the whole of your and your family's life revolves.

As one man who had been unemployed for four years put it: 'You've got to have a philosophy of life, and mine is you've got to make the best of your life.' This is John, unskilled and with a disabled wife, an energetic toddler and a sick baby. Being at home on long-term supplementary benefit is indeed a fair way of making the best of life for them. Not without its fair share of ups and downs, but as good a deal as any (both for them and for society, when you consider the likely extra demands on the National Health Service were she unattended with him out at work all day). John recognizes that the paid work ethic is not for him. His ethic is adaptability and making do. Which after all is what the poor have always had to do.

There is evidence from recent researches that after about a year, the physical and psychological health of the unemployed does not continue to deteriorate and tends to improve slightly. Twelve months is the point at which the financial gravity of their situation often sinks home and people have to start making major adaptations in lifestyle. The improvement in health may well be associated with acceptance of one's unemployment. (This improvement has only been noticed recently, because up till recently researchers had looked only at health on becoming unemployed, not at the health of the long-term unemployed.)

If losing your job is experienced as some kind of bereavement, then our knowledge of other forms of bereavement indicates that it often takes about twelve months of grief to come to terms with the loss, and only after that can people accept that life is now going to be different and can they positively enter into that new life. Our knowledge of bereavement indicates that only when the loss is really accepted can life begin again. Clinging on to what has been lost (as the Job Centre leaflets encourage the unemployed to do) delays the whole process of coming to terms with the situation.

When you cease to believe that a job is just around the corner, then two things become possible. One is that you can come to terms with your situation.

Jim and Rhona live in a new town where unemployment is high. Jim is unskilled, and was frequently depressed during his first year of unemployment. After about a year, Rhona (who had given up her nursing training to get married and have their first two children, and who also has little hope of getting a job) said, 'Look Jim, we've got to buck up. This is the only family we're ever going to have, and I really want a third child. If we're going to make a success of that, we've really got to pull together.' From that point on, Jim accepted that he wasn't likely to get a paid job, and he and Rhona have put all their energy into running their family. Their third child, Katy, is now three and sat contentedly on Rhona's lap for much of the two hours I was talking with them, while the two older boys played happily in and around. As relaxed an atmosphere as any researcher could hope for when interviewing a family with three young children! What was remarkable was that this couple talked frankly, freely, and at length about their relationship and their life, with three young children running in and out. This family has got its act together as well as any you are likely to find. Certainly there are tensions and Jim still has his down times, but they have learnt how to handle them. All of this has been possible only because Rhona decided that Jim had to face up to being unemployed, and because they decided as a couple what it was they wanted out of their one and only life.

Both Jim and Rhona stressed one particular event: Jim's giving up gambling. He comes from a gambling family, and the decision to give it up came along with the decision to try for a third child. It seemed to me that the gambling had to do with the hope that sometime Jim's lucky number would come up — whether it be a paid job or a big win. Giving up gambling was part of Jim's acceptance that he cannot go through life relying on chance. Giving up gambling had to do with accepting the limits of life as it is, and setting about creating a predictable framework in which he and Rhona could *make* things happen rather than wait for fate to let things happen for them. For Jim, giving up both gambling and immediate hope of a paid job were not defeatism, but facing reality, and the first stage of his family taking control of its own life again. They sat down and worked out a budget, which it was now possible to do rationally because they could exclude the unpredictabilities of a big win or paid employment dropping by chance into Jim's lap.

This then is the second thing that becomes possible once you accept you are unlikely to get a job in the foreseeable future: you can feel confident about tomorrow, next week, next year.

For Jim and Rhona, this meant that they were freed to plan: plan their money, their resources, their time and their respective roles. For Pete, it means he is freed to take each day as it comes: 'I don't make plans, I just see what turns up each day.' This is why he is so able to work for others as and when the need arises, or to amuse himself as and when the mood takes him. There is none of the 'Oh, I can't promise to help, I've got an interview on Wednesday and may be in work next week'.

In chapter 10 of his book *Workless,* Dennis Marsden describes several skilled men he met who spent a remarkably busy unemployment, painting or making jewelry in the potting shed in the back garden. Indeed their informal work was in every respect save money far more creative and satisfying than the paid work they had been forced to leave. Few if any of them, however, could accept this situation, and were actively looking for paid work. They ended up taking paid jobs with worse pay and conditions than their previous paid job, and clearly had mixed feelings about this. None of them got to the point of accepting their unemployment and deciding to make the best of their lot. The tragedy is that they felt they had to return to the formal economy and sell their souls to the industrial system.

So it is possible to be active when unemployed, even though you do not accept your unemployment. But it is not possible to make the most of this activity; nor does it bring contentment.

Samantha was unfairly dismissed from her job as a radiographer, and ended up moving to Wiltshire, where she bought a seventeenth-century house and did it up. This was hard and satisfying work, and was financially profitable when she sold the done-up product, yet she still did not feel it to be 'a job' and stressed to me how traumatic she found this period of unemployment. She could not relish her home-made work even though it was more satisfying than her previous work; she felt unemployed and unable to accept such a condition. She is now happy, selling houses for a large developer, with a salary sufficient to enable her to enjoy the beautiful cottage she has now moved to.

Accepting the fact of your unemployment may not be easy, given the conventional wisdom that unemployment is a terrible thing. It is perhaps easier to accept if you have a supportive spouse who also accepts it, like Rhona. It can also be easier if, like Pete, you are single and do not have the hassle of having to convert your family to your point of view.

Ray Pahl has suggested that social support also varies enormously from place to place. If you live in an area dominated by the work ethic, such as white-collar suburbia or a traditional, skilled-blue-collar council estate, it may be very difficult to

stability in a marriage. When the husband in such a marriage becomes unemployed, the tensions can quickly mount. The wisest course of action here may be for the husband to find something to do outside the house, whether it's pottering in the potting shed or joining the local darts team. Jack, who lost his job in the steel industry four years ago, described how dire things got between him and his wife Marjorie, 'I was just pacing up and down and wearing a groove this deep in the carpet.' Marjorie confirmed that their marriage had nearly broken up. Salvation had come in the form of a community workshop run by an amalgamation of local churches, providing tools and a workshop for anyone, employed or unemployed, who wishes to use it. Jack and his eleven-year-old son spend a lot of time down at the workshop now, and they showed me the joinery work they are currently engaged on. 'If it weren't for that place, I don't know whether we'd still be together,' said Marjorie.

Other marriages, however, may thrive on having the man around more; certainly this is why some couples look forward to retirement. Some young families also thrive on having the father around more. Whereas married women with children under five are less likely than other women to have a paid job, married *men* with under-fives are more likely to have a paid job and fathers of large families work more overtime than other men (Rimmer and Popay, *Employment Trends and the Family,* pp. 49—51). It is precisely when there are young children at home that men spend most time out of the house earning a living. Rimmer and Popay suggest that there should be less concern about the effect on children of working mums, and more concern about working parents and in particular working fathers. It is their fathers that young children do not see, not their mothers.

Some of the unemployed recognize this. One couple interviewed on 'Woman's Hour' recently commented that an advantage of being unemployed was that they could meet their four children's needs by spending time with them and doing things together, whereas they felt that many other children tended to have their childish desires met by parents spending money on them and not by passing time with them.

Arthur and Angela had their second and third child within a year. Angela readily admits that, though she loves children, she's not too keen on babies, and that Arthur did most of the baby care for the first couple of years. This was possible because he was unemployed. They shared the getting up in the night, two nights on, two nights off. Angela is very thankful that she did not have to experience what her sister went through when she had three babies close together while her husband was away most of the time working in Iran. Unable to afford a phone, and with all the public phones on the estate vandalized, Angela is glad she is not alone with three young children. She talked of how women on their own with children have scrimped and saved to keep the phone, for fear of having to leave the children alone to walk the streets at night in search of a phone to call the doctor.

However, this reversal-cum-sharing of roles was not permanent and, now the children are eleven, five and four, things are more conventional. Whereas Arthur defines himself as unemployed, Angela was horrified when I asked if she saw herself the same way, 'No! I'm a housewife!' Arthur has been depressed and suffers from severe headaches, which Angela is convinced are related to his unemployment.

Likewise John and his epileptic wife Deirdre by no means fully or permanently share roles. John is averse to the more work-like aspects of child-rearing such as nappy-changing, and is often out of the house doing odd jobs for people and helping with a local political party. Brewing beer and erecting a garden fence are the kind of homely tasks he talks of with most relish.

I met only two couples who have really made child-rearing their joint career. One couple on Merseyside simply thrive on each new child, and now have ten. It is one of those large, happy families where the children seem to look after each other. The living room contained, I think, all ten when I visited plus the parents, yet somehow did not seem crowded. A lot of people but nobody seemed to be getting on top of each other. Dad is one of the 3 per cent who could not possibly find a job paying anything like as much as they get on the dole, yet I went away feeling they were contributing to our society. Certainly I would rather be a child growing up in this family than in one of those many families where there is a father dutifully paying his taxes who I never see and a mother who doesn't enjoy being stuck at home.

Jim and Rhona are the other couple remarkable for the jointness of their 'operation parenthood'. Apart from time spent on their allotment, they are together virtually the whole time. They have no car and, for those without a car, their new town is pretty much a remote island, being one of those 1960s planning dreams premised on the motor car. Near a motorway it may be, but not near much else.

They are disarmingly frank about the stresses of being together twenty-four hours a day. 'It affects playtime,' Rhona volunteers, 'you don't feel so amorous if you've been looking at each other all day.' Nor is it easy when Jim gets depressed. Rhona, who seems the expert and leader in personal relationships in the household, forces him to talk by threatening to go and stay with her mother. Jim is genuinely appreciative. Every six months or so there is a big bust up, but they are careful not to row in front of the children, and they both know it's frustration about the limitations of having so little money and being on top of each other rather than actual anger at the other person. They both agree that unemployment has been a boon for their relationship, which is now much more open, sharing and caring.

They both accept each other. He accepts her organizing their life and readily admits that she has changed him, for the better; he appreciates the way she never lets feelings fester below the surface. She, for her part, accepts and appreciates him, whether or not he's got a paid job. 'I've never said to you, "You're not worth anything because you've no job," have I?' and Jim's reaction indicated to me that he knew that not only had she never said it, she had never felt it either.

The openness includes the three children, two boys of about

nine or ten, and three-year-old Katy. One of the boys wanted a computer, and Rhona and Jim had to explain that neither of them had a job and it was a choice between a computer and food. Rhona admitted that one of the boys really got to her when he said, 'But you smoke, Mum.' She knows this is her one extravagance; she finds it helps her to relax. Anyway, she cut down as part of the 'no computer deal', and puts the money saved into a kitty for occasional outings.

They both stressed that bringing up a family on the dole is no picnic. In fact, they almost seemed to take a pride in the fact that it was a struggle, a struggle that brings them all closer together. (Shades here of Seabrook's version of the old working class pride in making do and how it brings people together. Here, however, it is not a community but a family that is united through a shared struggle.)

They insist that the key to their success is good management. Their finances are budgeted to the last penny. Golden rule number one is never to get into debt. They reject hire purchase, and save up for things. Every week it is absolutely essential that a fixed amount goes into 'my little pot of gold' as Rhona puts it, a kitty from which they can buy things when they are cheapest: like next winter's clothes in the spring sales. It then also becomes possible to snap up a bargain at an auction or get the superb kitchen unit that a neighbour was selling for a song. The result is a beautifully furnished home and well turned-out kids.

Rhona is self-conscious about the apparent affluence of their home, because this fruit of their immaculate budgeting has caused some nasty comments from neighbours, and even from her parents, who seeing the video and the new fridge-freezer say, 'Aye, aye, it's all right for some, living a life of luxury on the dole.' This has lost them friends, throwing them even more on each other, and has caused them much pain. 'They don't see the struggle and everything we have to forego to live like this,' Rhona says. They have worked very hard for it all, and yet get accused of getting it for free off the state. In fact, they take a pride in not asking for the special payments to which the long-term unemployed are entitled from time to time to meet exceptional needs, such as the replacement of a cooker. She feels the new class barrier that is emerging between the employed and the unemployed.

The video they feel is a boon. If a child is about to watch an unsuitable programme in the evening, the potential conflict is easily sidestepped by saying, 'Your dad recorded your favourite cartoon programme this morning. Would you like to watch that?' For a family thrown together, with little or no money for expensive pursuits, the video definitely helps both the quality of entertainment within the home and the parents' ability to control the little box in the corner rather than have it control them or their children.

They make a point of having a holiday once a year. Once they went camping, and another time they shared a luxury eight-berth caravan with her parents, which they said worked very well.

Financially, they are fortunate in two ways. One is that they have at least one close relative who is not unemployed, and on occasion they can borrow her car. This enables occasional outings and occasional bulk-buying shopping trips. They are also lucky that they are only a few minutes trolley push from the main shopping precinct, which has a good range of cheap shops and a permanent market. Certainly the prices amazed me.

Jim would take a job if one turned up that paid enough to live on. But he does not feel any loss of male pride in working in the home: 'Most men don't know the work involved in bringing up a family.' So he is far from being a shirker, either in the household or the formal economy outside. Were he to take a paid job I almost feel it would be a shame, they are making such a good job of bringing up the children together.

I have talked about Jim and Rhona at length because they made a joint decision not to let unemployment get in the way of what they wanted out of life, and indeed in a way turned it to their advantage. I consider them to be an impressive family. More commonly the decision to accept unemployment as an opportunity to invest more energy and time in homemaking is a decision by and for the mother. I think of Joanna, who worked to support her husband when he was at college during the early years of their marriage. She worked on and off as the first two children came along, and strongly felt she wanted to keep on the ladder of her chosen career of nursing, to which she is strongly committed. They have recently moved to an African country where financial and cultural pressures against working women are even greater than in Britain, and now with the birth of their third child she has decided to make the best of the situation. She wrote to me:

> I'm enjoying being at home these days. Although it's a lot of work I really believe that my kids should be brought up by me and not a nanny which is the done thing here. I have plenty of years to go back to my nursing.

She seemed to have turned unemployment into mothering, to her satisfaction at least for the time being. The next letter, however, indicated that they could not make do without her taking some kind of paid work, and Joanna has found a way of combining mothering with earning some money:

> We're finding it more and more difficult to cope with only one salary. So next term I'm starting up with my teaching piano lessons . . . I have about ten people already lined up. There's a real shortage of piano teachers, so I don't think I'll have any problems getting students. I just hope it works out with the babe around. Anyway, we'll see how we go.

Though some women like Joanna may come to terms with increased involvement in household and community, we have no right to assume that all women will feel the same. Though unemployed women do not have the anxiety of unemployed men about it being cissy to be at home and though women do usually respond to unemployment by enlarging their role at home, Angela Coyle's warning must be heeded:

> Unemployment for women is often experienced as a crisis of

autonomy, as a loss of independence, and here women's domestic role is no compensation. On the contrary, work for women has been their route *out* of domestic and financial dependence. Consequently, the family may soften the blow of job loss, but in the end the family appears to be the trap.

There are many unemployed who are forced into a closer involvement with their families that they would rather not have; and there are many employed who would rather spend more time with their families. Surely a civilized society can arrange its affairs a bit better, so that those parents at home are the ones who want to be at home? The benefits for our children could be enormous.

Politics and sport

Parenting is not the only full-time occupation which you do not get paid for, which has to be financed somehow, and for which the dole may be a useful source of finance if there are no other possibilities. One other such occupation is local politics. Originally this was the preserve of the gentry, who had both time and money to serve the community in this way. Nowadays, it really is not possible to take a major role in local politics, say by chairing a committee of a county council, unless you are financially supported in some way or other. This usually means one of two things: being a middle-class wife with a second car and a husband's income sufficient for the whole family to live on, or having an employer who is happy to give you a lot of time off. Some councillors who have been made redundant from their job have taken the opportunity to take on more responsibility on the council; but this is an opportunity to be grasped immediately, before declining funds force the disposal of the phone and the car, without which it must be pretty difficult to be an effective local councillor, especially in a rural area.

Another full-time occupation for which there is no payment is amateur sport at its higher levels. This too was originally the sole preserve of the gentry. No one with only one day off a week

142

could hope to climb high in a time-consuming sport such as cricket. Another sport, which has to this day remained almost entirely amateur in Britain, is mountaineering. This was pioneered in the 1850s and 1860s by gentlemen of leisure who had the time and money to spend their summers sitting out the Alpine storms awaiting a fine day for an assault on the Weisshorn or the Dent Blanche. Clergymen of the Church of England seemed particularly endowed with the necessary time. Not until the depression of the 1930s did the working class have the time to start their own form of mountain climbing. The unemployed of Sheffield and Glasgow found the hills close enough not to require expensive travel, and they set off in considerable numbers. Tom Weir, a regular correspondent for the *Scots Magazine* recalls the days of his youth:

> What I remembered was the idealism of the 1930s, this despite the depression and the dole. The men I knew then sought the countryside, carrying everything on their backs and taking a fierce delight in the art of being comfortable with the minimum of kit, dossing in bothies, caves, or under shelter stones, knowing how to light fires with wet wood and carrying no more than newspapers or a single blanket for sleeping. Quite a number came back to Glasgow, only to sign on at the Labour Exchange, pick up their dole and go off again exploring.

Pete and his kids use the dole for just this kind of opportunity, but the tradition has not, to my knowledge, been extensively revived during the present recession. There are, however, some other sportsmen and women who have reason to be grateful for unofficial funding by the dole. I mean amateur athletes.

I have already quoted from the local newspaper hailing the hard-working life on the dole of Olympic hopeful, Trevor Lyons. Trevor had landed an MSC job at the local university gym, but was getting rather frustrated because he was being used simply to sweep up and clean the loos; knowing he had more talent than most of the students who used the gym, relations with his boss got worse and worse. Eventually his dad, who is a voluntary coach at Trevor's local athletics club, found out what was troubling his son and decided Trevor should give up the job. In the two years since then, Trevor has been training on the dole, six hours every day, with tremendous support from father and girlfriend, who is also a gymnast. The support is financial as well as moral. The cost of gear cannot be met from the amount of dole received, and Mr Lyons was forever chauffering Trevor to training sessions and events around the country. Recently this has involved a regular dash a hundred miles up the motorway to the national training centre near Birmingham. Because of the pressure on Mr Lyons' time, he has recently bought Trevor a car, which was no small sacrifice for the Lyons' family finances.

Quite simply, unless you are supported by income from a landed estate, by well-off parents, an interested employer such as the Armed Services, or an American University, there is little chance of a young hopeful getting into the Olympic team unless he goes on the dole. Trevor is lucky because he has support from his parents and the local community, and the implicit support of the local DHSS. Others are not so lucky. I suspect our national athletics performance along with our child-rearing suffers from our perverse reluctance as a society to fund without strings those people who recognize and wish to develop their own natural talents. The loss to our society's true wealth by this inhibition of talent is immense. Hurray for Rhona and Jim and Trevor who simply get on with what they are good at, with or without the permission of the DHSS!

Community work

Another traditionally unpaid job is good works in the local community. This was once the preserve of the lady of the manor, then of the middle-class wife whose children had grown up and who was supported by her husband. Now there is a new form of local voluntary worker: the 'community worker' funded on a shoestring by a charitable organization or by the MSC, or done unofficially on the dole, or with the worker supporting him or herself by part-time work. Often such workers have voluntarily given up more lucrative jobs. I think of those training for a professional career who have become disillusioned, finding that the role of medicine or social work or architecture is much less altruistic than they had once fondly imagined, or those in manual jobs who have become fed up with the brutality of their work.

Indeed, some modern missionary work is being done on the dole. In one large northern city, a young Anglican layman, with the support of other local churches, lives off a mixture of dole and adult education teaching and has moved into a notorious estate, with flats housing 9,000 people, to start a church, based in his own flat. He has a passionate belief that it is in such areas, usually written off as 'deprived', that hope for our world is to be found. He writes,

> In the place where black and white live cheek by jowl and where racial prejudice sometimes spills out into the light of day, racism can be overcome . . . In a structure which isolates neighbour from neighbour a new community can grow. There cannot be hope without hopelessness and there cannot be resurrection without crucifixion.

He feels strongly that a religion based on a poor man preaching to the poor in a remote backwater of the Roman Empire gives great hope that it is among the poor that we are most likely to find God today:

> Here is where the lion lies down with the lamb and justice flows down like streams of living water. I have seen a black rastafarian and a white racist youth spend a happy evening together discovering their commonness in music; I have met a doddery old lady who lives on her own — who for a few years has daily fed and nursed a senile neighbour. I have seen fervently at prayer together a white Catholic and a Black pentecostal woman; and so I could go on.

It is not a matter of doing good to the poor, but of living with them and learning; and to be poor with the poor may well mean being unemployed.

This young man seems to be taking on the traditional role of the parish priest for the kind of community that the Church's clergy and their wives are not usually keen to be sent to. As the Church of England's cash runs short, the dole may come to supplement the Church Commissioners for funding that long-established community worker, the local vicar.

Not only some missionaries but also para-military organizations in Northern Ireland are largely funded by the DHSS. Here is an intriguing example of people deciding to take control of their own lives, even though they are denied a paid job. Sinn Fein has set up a comprehensive network of local advice centres, where people in disadvantaged areas can come for support and advice with problems concerning their pension or the local housing department. The centres arrange transport for old people and offer other services as need arises. They are staffed mainly by young adults drawing the dole who are motivated by deeply held political or religious beliefs. (Fryer and Payne noted that this is a feature of those they studied who live actively while unemployed.) There appears to be a dedication among the Sinn Fein workers that one does not always find among professional politicians and social workers, and they claim this to be a factor in their popularity. In other words, they work harder at community work than many of those paid to do it and trained at considerable expense to the taxpayer. This indeed seems to be a feature of much voluntary work. It is perhaps embarrassing to those who disapprove of Sinn Fein's community workers that they are motivated by higher values than the money which motivates most law-abiding paid employees.

Other forms of community work may seem to the taxpaying employee not so much subversive as unreal. Just as it is easy to dismiss the twin-set do-gooder as having too much time on her hands and nothing better to do, so it is easy to dismiss the new-style community worker as playing while we (the real workers with real jobs) have to run the real world. But such people can and do play a valuable role in enabling neighbourhoods to thrive, especially where there is not the natural community of a Coronation Street, nor middle-class wives, nor a minister of one of the established churches.

Further education

Involuntary unemployment may spell the end of a career in which considerable time and commitment has been invested. Some change of course will be necessary, but where to go next? If a wise decision is to be made, horizons have to be widened, so that the person can become aware of the full range of options and explore personal talents that had hitherto lain undeveloped. In other words, some kind of further education is often necessary.

However, grants may not be available for this. There was perhaps a time when it was possible to work part-time in order to pay your way through college, but such work may not be available now. To be officially registered as unemployed, but unofficially studying full-time may be the answer.

If a course is largely peopled by such students, it may have difficulty escaping the eye of a watchful local social security office. I think of one particular residential course where most of the students have little money. Technically, you are not allowed to draw the dole and be studying more than twenty-one hours a week, and tuition fees are not payable by the DHSS (though rent is). So the course is advertised as containing only sixteen hours of formal lectures a week; students on the dole are let off tuition charges, but accommodation is charged fully to all students because this can be recouped by the poorer ones from the DHSS. This course seems to have been particularly effective in giving a stream of students over the years a sense of direction and commitment to serving their fellow human beings. As far as society is concerned, it is good value for money as it is enabling these people to live up to their potential and so add to the real wealth of society.

Hobbies

Some people use unemployment not so much to explore new avenues as to develop some long-standing interest. For youngsters on one estate in Bath the thing is to buy up an old banger of a car or motorbike for not much more than a fiver, and spend every daylight hour tinkering with it with your mates. This is a very social activity, and you can often see a crowd of youngsters around some machine that is in a thousand and one parts.

Arthur, whose paternal instincts we have already observed, was trained as a grill chef. With the recession, there are not nearly so many people on Merseyside eating out, and he has little chance of a job now. His passion is miniature-rose breeding, and the back garden of his council house resembles nothing so much as a miniature and rather less windswept version of the Liverpool Garden Festival. Arthur, however, does not have £30 million backing! What rose breeding really requires is not money, however, but time and patience, which Arthur has in abundance. There is interest from one or two commercial sellers, and Arthur is likely to be paid several hundred pounds should he develop a breed that is commercially viable. He wonders whether, if he produces two or three successful breeds, it might be possible to go into business properly. His wife, Angela, is not so sure about that, but she is very proud of his horticultural achievements to date.

In the meantime, Arthur has been offered a £76 a week gardening job on an MSC programme. With three young kids, Angela — an evangelical Christian — feels it simply isn't worth it. He's better digging pensioners' gardens for free as he does at present, even though he does not enjoy being unemployed. When the youngest child is five and at school next year, Angela thinks it would be financially worthwhile if both of them could get a job. But just now they are in the poverty trap, where wages for an unskilled (!) man like Arthur are barely enough to support a family without additional part-time earnings from the wife. Just now, there are two realistic options:

Both Arthur and Angela might take low-paying jobs, if they can find jobs, and pay a child-minder.
They could both stay at home, Arthur on the dole.

As we have already seen, the children are going to miss out on one or both parents with the first course of action, and are likely to flourish most on the second. In the long run, society too will benefit from three children who have not been starved of love. And a run-down part of Merseyside may get a rose named after it!

When I was unemployed, my writing could be seen as a time-consuming but inexpensive hobby. Like Arthur, I did not know whether or not it would lead to more employment; as it turned out, it led to self-employment. Unemployment gave me the chance to try my hand at writing more or less full-time. It did not really matter to me whether or not it led to anything that would bring me a living, for in the meantime I was both productive and fulfilled.

For the skilled unemployed that Marsden interviewed, most had some hobby or other — woodwork, artwork, photography, buying and selling art nouveau tea sets — and for many this brought in a little occasional undeclared income. Far from being an abuse, for many this kind of little fiddle was the only viable alternative to real crime. It was a way of supporting their family, or of being able to escape the house to go for a pint without having to take drinking money out of the household budget. Marsden comments:

Fiddling brought them once again the sense of control over their lives which some of them clearly valued in work. It brought money that was their own and not the state's or their wives' . . . Fiddling kept alive an individual's self-respect in the face of evidence that employers did not want him. Fiddling was a protection against the charge that he was 'doing nothing'. We conclude that for some of the workless in a very real sense fiddling was work.

For some, their hobby *is* crime. For the bored unemployed kid with nothing better to do, petty thieving may keep the day interesting and provide a little cash or goods in lieu. As far as motives are concerned, this may be no different from the way many of the unemployed are involved in rather more legitimate activities. Thieving and hobbies both pass the time and give you something to do.

There is a widespread view that unemployment leads some into crime, and therefore our society must provide more paid work if public order is to be maintained. It seems to me a sick society that so distrusts its members that it feels it must make them into wage slaves in order to keep them from getting into trouble with the law! If there is nothing legal for the unemployed youngster to do, then the fault can lie as much in lack of opportunity in the non-formal as in the formal economy. Surely it is because a society besotted with money has clamped down on opportunities in the non-money economies and is obsessed with controlling the black economy, that there is the common complaint of the delinquent, 'I was bored, and there was nothing better to do.'

For some of the unemployed, there is no one over-riding passion, but the day is well filled with a range of activities. John admits that boredom is the enemy and he takes active steps to beat it. Apart from sometimes looking after children and wife, he does local political work which includes door knocking and stamp licking for the local ward councillor, and he is active in the local Anglican church. He does some decorating for friends on the side, which produces the useful occasional tenner. He is a passionate reader of thrillers; buying them second-hand at ten pence each, he builds up complete sets of particular authors, and when he has read them sells them at fifty pence a copy to dealers who are looking for complete sets. 'It's not much, but every odd bob comes in handy.'

He's also had a go at amateur printing. He bought some fancy writing paper with a floral border, used Letraset characters to do the wording to invite people to their baby's christening, and then got it photocopied onto coloured card at the local Prontaprint shop. He enjoyed this and is hoping he'll be able to provide an informal service for any friends who want the same kind of thing done.

John is perhaps typical of many. Life has its share of problems, but he's cheery enough, and is involved in all three of the non-formal economies. Boredom and lack of money *is* a problem, but so it is for many with paid work too. Is he the ordinary working man of the future?

Small is beautiful

There is a problem with all this. It may be possible to write a book while on the dole, or breed roses, or look after old ladies, or bring up a family. But, there are many, many things that you cannot do on your own: teaching 'A' level chemistry, automobile manufacture, coalmining, roadmending, to name but four. It may be possible for the unemployed teacher to do private tutorial work, but he is handicapped without a school laboratory. A genius may be able to build a car out of spare parts, but it will be a pretty poor substitute for the latest model built by robots in Turin. In the 1930s, mining families scavenged from the local tip, and a few even reopened their own secret individual pits, but with scant reward for their labours. Roadmending requires a vast bureaucracy compared to the village rota of pre-industrial times. Before the agricultural enclosures and the industrial revolution, most jobs could be done by an individual, or by an individual family; there could be dire poverty, but unemployment did not really exist. Now, most jobs are highly industrialized and bureaucratized, and relatively few jobs can be done independent of the industrial/bureaucratic machine. The unemployed teacher I met who was frustrated that he could not use his skills and training is more typical than the unemployed author who can. The tragic fact is that most people need an employer if they are to exercise the skills they have been trained for.

Some of the 'alternative' writers, notably Ivan Illich, have understood this. They encourage us to develop skills that do not depend on the industrial bureaucratic system for their exercise. From organic farming to free schools to house churches, they advocate unilateral independence from the industrial/bureaucratic system. Whether or not one agrees with their critique of society as a whole, the lesson for the unemployed is clear. If there are no jobs in the formal economy, then see what skills you have or can develop that can be exercised independently from 'the system'. 'Small' may or may not be 'beautiful' for society at large; it is a necessity for the unemployed.[1] This is the virtue of the self-sufficiency movement. What is so unfortunate is that it is largely middle class and rural, divorced from the life of the urban working class unemployed. But there surely are a wide range of activities left undone in the cracks of our industrial system that can be done on a small scale. It is encouraging that E. F. Schumacher, the man who coined the phrase 'small is beautiful', was no Indian peasant but chief economic adviser to the National Coal Board.

[1] This is not to eschew all large organizations. The unemployed do benefit from the DHSS, the Department of Employment, and the MSC.

9 Money and Resources

Unemployment and supplementary benefit are calculated to meet people's physical needs. It is also assumed that a washing machine and television will be cheaper than going outside the house and buying someone else's services to launder and entertain your family. Beyond that, anything else is seen as a luxury by the DHSS.

However, benefits calculated on this limited notion of need expect people to sit at home, fed, clothed and housed, but with no spare money to enable them to lead an active life. In chapter 1, I argued that many so-called luxuries are used to capitalize activity, and without them most people are sentenced to a rather passive existence. A car, a phone, an electric drill or other tools, a ladder, a typewriter are investments for an active life.

There is an important contrast between the philosophy behind our present social security arrangements and current thinking in voluntary overseas aid agencies. A decade or two ago, there was an important shift in the philosophy of relief agencies such as Oxfam and Christian Aid. They began to realize that programmes that were no more than first aid for disaster zones simply made the recipients dependent. What was needed was to provide simple tools and skills so that people could start to look after themselves. The change is summarized in the slogan: 'Give a man a fish and you feed him for a day. Teach him how to fish and you feed him for a lifetime.' Well, our social security is still at the stage of giving people fish. What they need as well is to be given a fishing rod, so that they can begin to fish for themselves.

This means that at the very least the social security scales should include an element that enables people to capitalize self-chosen activity in the non-formal economies. This need not be an enormous quantity; an extra 15 or 25 per cent would make an enormous difference to the life of the unemployed.

With very few exceptions, the unemployed who lead an active, creative life are those who somehow or other have found this extra for themselves. When I started writing articles, an inexpensive activity if ever there was one, I still needed (1975 prices):

a second-hand typewriter, bought for £10 through an ad in the paper (I'm still using the same beautiful machine ten years later: an excellent investment!)

paper, carbons, biros, postage stamps

a course to learn how to type (£25)

the reservation charge for ordering books through the library.

I was lucky. I had some savings and cashed in a now useless occupational pension (about £1,000), and every now and then (being an academic) I was paid to go to job interviews. This provided free trips away; I lived in Aberdeen and my ageing parents lived 500 miles south where most of the jobs were, so visiting them would have proved impossible but for the free train rides. Without this financial good luck, I do not see how I could have led an active or sociable life. But really, the amount of extra cash or resources the unemployed usually need to capitalize themselves effectively is very little (just as it costs little to capitalize an Indian peasant to feed himself), and it is a sadistic society that refuses them it.

In this chapter, I will describe the various ways in which the active unemployed I met found extra resources to make possible their life of activity.

Extra cash

There are two forms of income over and above your regular benefit. One is any lump sum that you inherit on the day you become unemployed. This may consist of savings, cashed-in insurance policies, or a redundancy payment. Those made redundant from Port Talbot in 1980 who had worked thirty odd years there had a redundancy payment, a British Steel Corporation pension of about £45 per week, 90 per cent pay for the first year, and 80 per cent for the next six months; some converted this extra pay into an augmented pension. But they are without doubt the aristocracy of the unemployed. Apart from such instances, few have anything left to speak of after twelve months. The many who have for years oscillated between low-paid jobs and unemployment, enter unemployment with no spare cash at all.

Once you are signed on, the only further source of cash is to earn something extra on a regular basis. There are two legal ways in which this may be done. One is to work the earnings rule to the limit. Handbooks such as Dauncey's explain how this may be done. Travelling and other expenses involved in work may be deducted from earnings, and those on unemployment benefit can earn as much as they like on Sundays. Jim and Rhona discovered to their amazement another loophole. They heard that a neighbour's earnings as a part-time fireman were totally disregarded by the DHSS, so they went along to the local library to see what other occupations were exempt. They looked the regulations up in a welfare handbook and found that there were only two others: lifeboatmen and child-minding. Since there is no great call for lifeboatmen in mid-Lancashire, they realized it would have to be child-minding or nothing. Two thirds of your earnings as a child-minder are deemed by the DHSS to be for toys, food, nappies and other expenses of the job, so only one-third are counted as earnings. So, if you earn £18 in a week, only £6 is counted as income; if you are on supplementary benefit with its £4 limit, that means you will only be docked £2 of your £18 earnings.

Jim and Rhona have therefore done some occasional child-minding, with perhaps £10 coming in some weeks. They have considered trying jointly to make a living at it — it being the *only* occupation where you can gradually build up your earnings till you can resign the dole queue. But they say the trouble is there simply are not enough well-off parents in their town to pay the proper rate of £1 per child per hour. A charge of 60 pence is more normal, and for the last child they charged only 50 pence. This is a classic example of the trap many unemployed find themselves in: most of them live in communities that have not enough money to generate the demand for viable new businesses. Never mind, Rhona feels a great sense of triumph at having played the system at its own game, done something she enjoys (looking after children), helped out some neighbours who needed their children minded, and got a few quid into the bargain.

The other possible source of regular income is to work informally and get paid in kind. An unemployed gravedigger in a large city gives his services for free regularly tidying up a parish graveyard. The church is appreciative, but knows that any payment will be deducted from his social security, so they have put money regularly aside into a holiday fund, and this year he and his family were given a holiday to the Island of Iona.

Another man who was a churchwarden when he was made redundant from his job as a glazier found himself doing all sorts of jobs around the church, his practical skills coming in handy. He did a lot of work on the roof of the building, but felt rather exploited and taken for granted by the church. Individual church members also asked him to do odd jobs on their homes and were much more appreciative; they regularly dug items out of the freezer to give him in return. It was the only way he and his family got a Sunday roast. Some of these people encouraged him to set up in business as a jobbing builder. They understood how difficult it is slowly to build up business while on the dole, so for the bigger jobs they kept the money back until he formally went self-employed. In this way he built up experience and contacts, and also a tidy sum in credit.

An organizer of one project for the unemployed has unofficially formalized this means to self-employment. His scheme officially provides activities for the unemployed, but if anyone succeeds in earning any money through their labours this is banked quietly in a special account. Unofficially the person's name is pencilled in so that if he or she should progress to self-employment it is possible to draw out the banked 'earnings'. Three ladies, for example, discovered that outsize frilly underwear is difficult to come by, so they bought up outsize plain knickers and embroidered them, building up trade ᵗill after eighteen months they drew out their 'savings' and formally started a business. The beauty of this scheme is that it enables people to become self-employed who couldn't otherwise without breaking the earnings rule, providing them with cash just when they need it. This scheme is sailing pretty close to the legal wind, but there seems scope here for churches, other voluntary agencies, bank managers even, to open savings accounts of this kind for the active unemployed, drawable only on termination of unemployment.

Personal luck

What comes across time and again in talking with unemployed people is their sheer good or bad luck in having had previous spending and saving habits that either do or do not fit in with social security regulations. People in paid employment do not gear their finances toward the possibility of unemployment; indeed most people have not the faintest clue about social security regulations, and it comes as a surprise on signing on to find out how much or how little they're entitled to. I was very lucky. I had savings that were just below the supplementary benefit limit; I had earnings related unemployment benefit for the first six months (since abolished); I had no financial outgoings such as loans or hire purchase repayments apart from a young mortgage comprising mainly interest payment which was wholly payable by the DHSS; I had no children (whose true cost is underestimated by the DHSS); I had full central heating, for which there was an additional payment irrespective of it being cheaper to run than individual electric fires. None of this was planned, but the result was that this first period on the dole was financially sound. When eventually I moved south to a paid job, my flat in Aberdeen had risen in value considerably because the oil bonanza there had coincided with my period of unemployment, and I left the dole queue several thousands of pounds better off than when I joined it.

Others do not land on their feet, no more to their discredit than my soft landing was to my credit. Investment in hire purchase equipment, a loan on a car, or — most brutal of all — savings carefully built up for an old age, can be viciously penalized by social security regulations, leaving people stripped of their assets and bewildered.

It is also very much a matter of luck whether or not you find legally remunerative informal work. The churchwarden/builder was lucky. Though he lives in a not very affluent part of town, he happens to go to a church which attracts some of the more affluent members of that community; so it was that he knew people who had money and resources who, fortunately, also were sensitive about how to play the system at its own game. In fact, finding informal work can be as much a matter of luck as finding formal work. Rhona and Jim were lucky to stumble across the one legitimate source of considerable extra income, but unfortunate not to know people well off enough to pay it.

Family resources

Even if you are reluctant to ask them for cash, or they do not have it anyway, parents and parents-in-law, uncles, aunts, brothers and sisters may all have various resources which they can give or lend you. Rhona and Jim and their children can go for the occasional jaunt because Rhona's sister lends them her car. I think also of a single parent on social security who takes her children a hundred miles to her parents each school holiday; once a year also, they all pile into the parental Volvo and go off for a caravan holiday. Or there is athlete Trevor Lyons whose work is funded by the cash, transport and training from Dad and his girlfriend. These resources can make all the difference between a spartan existence on social security, and something a little bit better.

Whether such resources are available depends on two things. One is whether you have any relations with resources. Many unemployed, because they live in areas of high unemployment and low wages, may not be surrounded by affluent relations. The second is whether the relationship is such that you feel able to ask. Pride may deter you.

Communal resources

There are many ways in which resources owned by community organizations can add substantially to the standard of living of the unemployed. I have mentioned the workshop in Sheffield which virtually saved Jack and Marjorie's marriage. Though the salary of Alex, who runs it, has to be paid, the running costs are minimal. As we have noted (in chapter 1), the cost of many materials is going down and down, so it doesn't require much money to provide the materials to keep Jack and his boy happy for weeks. When I visited him at the workshop he was making a beautiful pine corner cabinet for their home, and reckoned it would take about three weeks in all. I asked Alex to cost the materials. He scratched his head and thought for a minute, 'about £10'. Not much for three weeks' contentment, but too much for Jack and Marjorie. How were they to pay for it? Jack and Alex grinned at each other, 'Penny down and a penny a week!' This surely is the 'Give a man a fishing rod . . .' philosophy come to Sheffield, sponsored by a group of churches because the DHSS still think only of giving people fish (or rather the government and those who voted for it will not allow the DHSS to think in any other terms).

Then there is Angela, also a beneficiary of her local church. Their third child came rather soon after the second, so she prayed about their imminent lack of baby clothes. Result: seventy-two dresses from fellow worshippers! She thought God can be a bit excessive at times.

A local video group in Skelmersdale do not find that equipment drops out of the sky quite so readily. They have a clapped-out old machine with which school children can get the hang of what is involved in making a video film, but for any serious work they manage, not always easily, to find a car to transport them the fifteen miles to Liverpool where they can use proper equipment, funded by the arts council. Because they cannot pay to use it, they are bottom of the priority list and have to use it overnight. But with the additional resource of a one-year MSC worker who has been a shop steward, has received higher education in the social sciences and generally knows how to get things out of the system, they usually manage to beg, borrow or buy equipment from somewhere or other.

Credit unions are a small but valuable way in which a poor community can spread around whatever financial resources it has. Credit unions flourish in the United States and in Ireland; Glasgow is one of the better endowed British cities with, I think, sixteen. A credit union is a community-organized bank for those who have no access to a bank, who are not used to saving, or who are ill at ease in the plush-carpeted office of a bank manager. Those unemployed who do have a bank nearby may decide it's too expensive, since they cannot keep the £50 or £100 minimum balance that is necessary to avoid bank charges.

The credit union I visited in the converted basement of a not very beautiful block of flats in Glasgow is open every Thursday evening and it works as follows. Ordinarily you can take out no more than is in your account. However, on joining you are immediately eligible for a negotiated loan at 6 per cent, and the union can take over debts. For example, if the magistrates order you to pay back a loan shark at £10 a week and you cannot manage that, the union may take over the debt and negotiate with you a rate, say £5 per week, that you can manage. By law, the union itself cannot go into debt, so loans may not be available say at Christmas or during the summer holidays when most members have drawn out their savings. The bus-driver and his wife who run this credit union consider it introduces both the idea, and the possibility, of thrift and budgeting to poor families whose financial life had hitherto been one of being pushed about from pillar to post by sharks, magistrates and officials. Any member can act as a bank-clerk on a Thursday evening. Whether as depositors or clerks, members begin to see how the world of money can be controlled by ordinary folk like themselves as well as by millionaires and DHSS officials.

The night I visited this credit union I was very impressed by the warm, cosy, quietly confident atmosphere. Customers chatted with the clerk, children pottered around happily. In the corner was a small food co-op, with food bought at the local cash-and-carry plus twopence for transport. The co-op is open every day, and is useful for pensioners who find it difficult to get to other shops. They come for the daily lunch club, and buy the odd tin, not too big a daily load to take home. It is their very own corner shop, staffed voluntarily and with cheaper prices.

Political luck

In addition to resources provided by local organizations such as churches, arts groups, credit unions and food co-ops, there are the resources available from the local authority. These vary enormously from area to area. Some authorities provide concessionary fares on buses for the unemployed, while others perversely restrict this facility to pensioners. South Yorkshire has a cheap fares policy of some fame, and a journey that would have cost me 50 pence in Bath was a tenth that in Sheffield. District and city councils can vary widely in the resources they devote to housing, and in whether municipal leisure and entertainment facilities subsidize the poor or the wealthy. Sheffield is deliberately gearing its library and leisure services toward the unemployed. Bath subsidizes opera for the wealthy, but the young unemployed have to pay to hire a football pitch.

Whether the unemployed have access to resources provided by the ratepayer depends very much on the political complexion of the local authority where you live. Sheffield has been Labour for longer than most people can remember, but it includes within its boundaries some affluent suburbs which are very highly rated and help pay for services for all sections of the city. The virtually free bus service and the £800 rates that a friend of mine has to pay on a fairly ordinary four-bedroom suburban house go together. Affluent commuters are under firm Labour control.

Knowsley, a district council in Merseyside, faces a very different situation. Knowsley consists almost entirely of people who are not well off, largely in outer perimeter, post-war housing estates. There simply is not the rate base to provide services. So if I were unemployed, I'd have access to more things and be able to live more cheaply in Sheffield than I would in equivalent housing in Knowsley.

Bootle/Southport on Merseyside is in another position again. Like Sheffield, it has both poor and affluent areas, but it is under the Conservative control of the better-off dwellers in suburban Southport. Bad luck if you're unemployed in Bootle.

Public expenditure cuts hurt the unemployed disproportionately. As they cannot afford to buy most things, they are more reliant on communally provided resources. This applies both to facilities directly provided by local or central government, like libraries and swimming baths and public transport; and to independent organizations such as arts groups maintained in part by government grants. 'The market' may or may not be a more efficient way of producing goods and services for consumers with money, but it simply excludes those without money. The present government is hitting the pockets of the unemployed not just by keeping social security payments down, but also by cutting back on everything else as well.

Geographical luck

Geographical luck also plays an important part. Some communal facilities are free, by courtesy of the good Lord. The beaches at Swansea and, for those with transport, the Gower Peninsula are far from empty on a sunny May weekday; for unemployed steel workers, the Gulf Stream and a south facing beach may be no bad substitute for the Spanish or Bermudan beaches frequented by the lucky few whom BSC did not make redundant. On the train through South Wales, I frequently saw boys and men fishing in gravel pits and rivers. It is often forgotten that a large number of British industrial towns are located by the sea, and many of the others are on a river. Whether the beach is warm (West Hartlepool is not Swansea), or the river clean, is another matter.

The other major free resource is the countryside. The cotton and wool towns of Lancashire and Yorkshire are in intimate contact with the moors. A plod uphill out of such a town can take you on to the open moor and out of sight of the chimneys within a mile or two.

There is also climatic luck. To be unemployed in an old terraced street in the summer, when you can sit out on the step American style and chat with the passers-by, offers the possibility of developing a social life not entirely unlike that of eighteenth-century Bath! Certainly I have never felt more in tune with the sociable past of my adopted city than when wandering one day through the city centre with an unemployed skinhead who stopped every fifty yards or so to chat with someone or other. To be unemployed in a high-rise flat in Edinburgh in April, however, with the snow flurrying around, is to be denied any kind of free social life in the street. To be unemployed anywhere in Britain in January denies you this.

On yer bike again?

Some places have more free bounties of nature than others. Others have better bargains in the supermarket. Employers often recognize the increased cost of living in London and add a London weighting to the nationally agreed wage rates. There is no London weighting for those on the dole. The social security scales take all kinds of costs into account, but — apart from some housing costs — it is assumed it costs the same to live anywhere in Britain. It doesn't.

We have already seen that in some really run-down estates, the cost of living may be atrociously high. So it is also in isolated rural areas, where there is one village shop and one bus a week. However, some regions are cheaper — the north-west, for one — and this can offset expenses for the poor such as vandalism or a Conservative local council. By my reckoning, food in Scotland costs 10—15 per cent more than in England; to feed a hungry family on one of Glasgow's peripheral housing schemes is grim if you are on social security.

I have also mentioned that, if a significant number of people in an area are to be involved in the informal and black economies, there must be a vibrant demand for, as well as supply of, a wide range of services. If you are all unemployed steel workers, it may prove difficult getting an informal exchange of skills going (I'll mend your plumbing if you look after my kids for the day). In more mixed areas, where there are solicitors and accountants as well as unemployed painters and decorators, the informal economy is more likely to work for the benefit of the unemployed. When I was on the dole, I got some very valuable free legal advice from a solicitor neighbour in return for letting him store some furniture in my garage. In a more uniform town, there would be no way I could get legal advice without paying for it.

Guy Dauncey laments the passing of the local economy, where local businesses respond to local demands. Nowadays the fortunes of a local company depend more on dictums from London or Houston than on the skills and demands of the local area. All too often a factory closes down even though there is nothing wrong with either it or the local workforce. Dauncey argues that, national policy apart, local communities can generate their own new businesses. This is surely true, but it is much truer of some areas than of others. It is relatively easy to find both a market and the required labour force for a new business in the mixed community of Bath or many of the older market towns, but in places not much smaller, such as Kirkby on the outskirts of Liverpool or Drumchapel on the outskirts of

Glasgow, there simply is not the money or the variety to generate anything more than a handful of new enterprises, formal or informal.

There are certainly some places where it is easier and cheaper to be creatively unemployed, and others where everything is against you. It is a complicated picture, though, and most places have both pluses and minuses. As an owner-occupier near the middle of Bath, I managed okay during my second period on the dole; had I occupied a council house on the outskirts, I'd far rather have lived in Sheffield.

It has been suggested that someone write a *Which?* guide to the best place to be unemployed, and I've heard of one person at least who moved to Sheffield, not because he'd have more chance of being employed 'but because he'd be better off unemployed there. But just as there can be severe penalties incurred in moving house to find better employment (see chapter 3), so the same penalties afflict any who move to find better unemployment: loss of friends and support (especially important for families with segregated roles), loss of contacts for finding work (in the informal as well as the formal economy). The unemployed are probably more in need of social support than the employed, and it can be difficult building this up without job or money. The only advantage is likely to be that housing will be cheaper and easier to find, but that may trap you should you later want to move to a job in a more expensive area. I would not advise anyone to get on their bike in search of good unemployment any more than in search of employment.

Avoiding money

Working for cash or kind, and making use of communal or family resources, are all ways of adding cash or resources to the basic dole. The other basic method for releasing more resources for yourself and your family is to develop skills that sidestep the money economy altogether: grow your own food, make your own clothes, and you should have cash spare from a dole which supposes you have to buy such things. Develop hobbies and interests that require no money or very little.

The model that immediately comes to mind here is that of Tom and Barbara in the TV programme *The Good Life,* and one regularly reads in the alternative press of couples living just like that. There was a tradition in the early industrial towns of workers keeping a pig or some hens in the back garden or yard, in much the same way as their agricultural parents or grandparents had done. The tradition has lasted into the twentieth century, and a Leeds city councillor tells me that every now and then there are complaints from someone that their neighbour is keeping a horse in their council house garden or garage, and did the council know that it is grazed every evening on the local school playing field!

However, this is very much the exception. Not everyone is into gardening and fewer still into keeping livestock, even though an old nag may save on bus fares; it is not that practical anyway should you chance to live on the sixteenth floor. How then do people sidestep the cash economy if they are living in a vast city and have no garden?

John admits to getting depressed with nothing to do, 'but I can still have a drink — brew my own'. With beer at 70 pence a pint down at the local, that is no small saving. Angela says she was useless at sewing at school but just happened to be fortunate that someone taught her later, and now she makes a lot of the children's clothes. A Merseyside family of ten have their birthday and Christmas presents made for them by their father out of scrap wood. They are a lot sturdier and more repairable than most bought toys (which they need to be with the possibility of ten consecutive young owners!). Though I wrote earlier that their house did not feel crowded, it was a bit hazardous not tripping over all the toys.

Pete gave by far the most extraordinary example of how to avoid the modern cash economy, even in the midst of the concrete jungle. Like the first inhabitants of the northern industrial towns, he too grew up in the countryside and first worked as a farm labourer before moving to the city. He took me round his own local wilderness, within 200 yards of his flat; this is a small scrubby wood, which most people would not look twice at. On a sunny August Saturday afternoon, he gave me a brief half-hour guided tour, and we didn't meet a soul; the growth was so luxuriant that we were not even aware of the tower blocks nearby. He inspected a large stand of wild raspberry canes, and reminded himself to remember this autumn to cut them back so that they bear some decent fruit next year. He then gave me some tips on surviving in the wilds, the sort of tips he imparts to the kids when he takes them camping. 'You can boil up the top leaves of nettles for tea, while every part of the dandelion is edible or drinkable: the flowers you can make wine from, the leaves you can cook as spinach, and the roots you can roast for coffee.' How do you roast in the wild? I asked. Simple. He showed me a small hole in the ground, rather like the entrance to a rabbit burrow, 'Take a hole like this, place the roots in an old tin, light a fire around it, and it'll take about an hour.' As for berries, he doesn't read books to find which are edible. He just eats one and sees how he feels afterwards. I began to see why his trips cost only a pound a day, as opposed to the £100-a-week school trips, and why the kids learn so much with him. This surely is self-sufficiency at its purest: opening our eyes to whatever resources happen to lie around us. It's an attitude of mind, I would say, more than a particular set of skills.

This attitude was not confined to the wilds. If Pete wants something, he usually has no difficulty getting or buying it. If it costs more money than he has, he simply goes without other things. He budgets to pay the rent on the TV and video, and the electricity, and if he's short at the end of the fortnight before the giro comes, he simply goes without food. When he moved into his present flat, he got a grant from the social security for furnishings; he spent this on a computer which then became his main source of amusement. Pete did not strike me as an ascetic, nor as an 'alternative' person. He simply does what he wants and/or what other people ask of him. He is very straightforward, and there is no fancy rhetoric.

All these ways of avoiding the cash economy are solo efforts. To make use of other people's skills, skill-swaps have been set up in some places. One such in South Wales involves no strict accounting and there is no rule that you have to put in as much as you get out. People like the work which gets them out of the house and gives them a sense of pride, and — unlike much work in the informal economy — it has the approval of the local DHSS because no money actually changes hands. Nor is there any antagonism from the trades unions, because the customers are all on social security and otherwise could not afford to get the work done, so no work is being taken away from tradesmen.

In fact, everything described in this section is legal. Social security and tax regulations have been devised to collect revenue in a money-based economy, and are simply not geared to self-sufficiency and barter. Work of this kind is neither legal nor illegal; it simply sidesteps the whole legal framework of a capitalist society. I would not argue that the future is to be found in self-sufficiency and barter, which are clearly inflexible in many ways. There is a limit to what can be produced and exchanged in this way; I cannot barter a joint of lamb for ⊃0 kilowatt hours of electricity. But for the unemployed who have that precious commodity, time, a judicious mixture of self-sufficiency, barter and bargain-hunting improves their standard of living considerably.

Dropping in

If poverty is 'a standard of living so low that it excludes and isolates people from the rest of the community', then one way of not becoming poor is simply not to mind being excluded from the rest of the community. Marsden observed: 'Only drop-outs — who had little financial or domestic stake in society and who disapproved of conventional expenditures on supermarket food, neat clothing and consumer goods — expressed any satisfaction with the levels of supplementary benefit payments.' Pete would fit this, though I'm not sure I would call him a drop-out, for he doesn't appear to be reacting *against* anything.

Fryer and Payne found that those who enjoyed an active life on the dole often held strong personal beliefs relatively independently of the society around them. Being true to themselves and what they knew about themselves or life or God was more important than being accepted by their fellow men and women. They were often very strong and impressive people. Far from being drop-outs, these are simply people with such firmly held values, and activities based on them, that material goods and being accepted simply fade into insignificance. One would hardly call Mother Teresa a drop-out. In my travels around Britain, I have found more dedicated artists, missionaries and parents with this attitude to possessions than hippies.

The ex-shop steward in Skelmersdale who had come across the counter culture during his sociological studies was scathing of those he sees as 'dropping out on the dole — they're still living in the 1960s!' All I can say is that none of those I have met living creatively and without poverty on the dole struck me as dropping out. Rather they are dropping in, to values and activities, which many employed people could do well to consider.

Investing in the poor: a proposal

None of the major political parties are anywhere near supporting a no-growth economy as advocated by some radical ecological thinkers. They are all committed to growth and to an economy based on money rather than self-sufficiency. Accepting this, there are some simple policy changes which could be made straightaway that would vastly improve both the lot of the unemployed and the real wealth of the nation. All that has to be done is to increase the money and resources going to the unemployed so that they can be released for productive activity in the non-formal economies, whether or not they are seeking paid work in the formal economy.

Without altering the basic framework of social security, three simple changes could be made:

1 Grant to those unemployed for more than a year the long-term supplementary benefit rate that all other categories of claimants are entitled to and that is acknowledged to be the minimum for a decent existence.

2 Enable the unemployed to earn more before benefit is withdrawn, as has already been done for single parents.

3 Include in the supplementary benefit rates an 'investment quota', say an extra 15 per cent. This is a sum intended not for subsistence but to capitalize activity. The claimant may then be able to install a phone, to buy a knitting machine or a typewriter, or to redecorate the house.[1]

These are very modest changes which could easily be made *within* the present framework of social security. Though they would cost the taxpayer a modest amount, they would result in valued goods and services being produced for the community, although most of these would not appear in the money-based figures of the Gross National Product. In the final chapter, I will outline a more radical set of proposals.

Let's look at how these modest proposals might work out in the case of Graham. Graham got into trouble at seventeen and, while at a hostel for young offenders, met the girl he ended up having to marry. After a few years she left him, and he is now twenty-two. He is a single parent with three children, lives on a council estate, and is on social security. He suffers criticism from neighbours and from the social services for leaving the

[1] This proposal does not mean that simply increasing current benefits by 15 per cent would of itself be satisfactory. Over the past few years, benefits for the unemployed have been cut below the levels agreed for physical subsistence, so a 15 per cent increase now would simply make good recent cuts. My proposal is to introduce a new *principle* into how the calculations are made, additional to making good any cuts or other deficiencies.

170

kids while he goes out for a pint or to go shopping for half an hour. So much so, that the social services are threatening to take the children away from him and place them in care. However, he has a real talent for mending things. He has fixed a one-armed bandit that the local community centre threw out, and it is now installed in his living room in all its splendour. The yard is full of bits of motor bikes which are his other passion. He is criticized further for spending too much money on his bikes and not enough on the children; he has to borrow money at high rates from money lenders, which is increasing his financial problems.

According to the local community worker, Graham is really a pretty good parent, but he does have difficulties reconciling himself to his lot in life. Any young tearaway who likes to consider himself hard would find it very difficult playing this 'soft' and supposedly feminine role. So Graham gets great pleasure and pride from excelling at football and table tennis, not to mention his biking activities. These are the very things that make him feel still like a man and enable his pride to allow him actually to spend most of his time looking after children. They are the very things that keep this family together.

Yet these are also the very things for which money is lacking. The community centre (along with its table tennis and football activities) is in danger of being closed down for lack of funds; and the mending of the bikes takes enough out of Graham's weekly giro to make it tight feeding and clothing the children.

What is likely to happen? Most likely, Graham will get deeper and deeper into debt, and the children will be taken away and cared for by the state, at great cost to the taxpayer. At great cost to the children too, who will most likely exchange a rather colourful dad, who does care for them, for a succession of foster homes. The other possibility, were one or more of the three minor policy changes above to be made, is that Graham would have just enough leeway to finance both what gives him a sense of identity (male sports and hobbies) and what he has been called to do (bring up his three children). He would be an asset

171

to his community, rather than the head of a 'problem family'. £10 a week is a small price to pay for all that. The alternative costs some hundreds of pounds a week directly, maybe much more indirectly, should the children grow up maladjusted.

If your response to this suggestion is 'Why should we, the taxpayers, pay for an irresponsible layabout like Graham?', then we must just agree to differ, for I have clearly not persuaded you of the main thesis of this book, that if taxpayers will not share out the paid work then they must give the unemployed every assistance to work informally. To have a social security system that is punitive toward Graham and the other three million unemployed families may do wonders for the sense of pride and self-righteousness of the taxpayer, but the loss to the real wealth of the community is enormous.

At the time of writing, there has been some debate as to whether or when Britain should start normalizing relations with the Argentinians and start investing in their economy again. These are the naughty boys of the international community, just as Graham (and the unemployed in general) are the naughty boys of the national economy. There is a very powerful argument that to send Argentina into some kind of international Coventry so that its economy collapses and it defaults on its debts is not going to be in the long-term interests of the international economy. Neither, surely, is it in the interests of British society or the British economy that the non-formal economies of the unemployed collapse for lack of investment. The only people who can pay for the subsequent repairs are taxpayers, and that *will* be a drain on the formal economy. In the end, the people we punish are ourselves.

Suffice it to say that the present government seems to be wanting to *reduce* benefits to the unemployed. It believes that high benefits make people dependent and are a drain on the community. The evidence points to exactly the contrary: it is *low* benefits that have these insidious effects.

10   Blessing in Disguise?

For many, unemployment has led to a turning point in their
lives. Unasked for maybe, but a turning point which they have
later come to value.

Unemployment is usually a crisis. The loss of paid work can
be a bereavement like losing your possessions in a fire or
burglary, losing your neighbours when moving house, or losing
your health. The loss of something that has been taken for
granted can be devastating, and occasionally people do not
recover. But generally people do recover. In *The Forsaken
Families* Leonard Fagin, a psychiatrist who studied the effects of
unemployment on family life, and his colleague Martin Little
wrote: 'The human capacity to survive a potentially destructive
experience and to create a different perspective on their situation
in order to achieve a mixture of positive and negative outcomes
for themselves, never ceased to amaze the researchers.' They
expected to find families traumatized for life, and found as often
families moving creatively in new directions.

When the carpet of normal life is taken from under you, one
way of rationalizing your unfortunate position is to question
whether 'normal' life is the only, or the best, life. It is not
unusual for those who have lost something or someone very
dear to ask themselves what is really important in life, and to
alter course accordingly. I remember the death of a very dear
friend, who had lit up the lives of many of her friends; I saw
then that writing books is rather unimportant in the light of
eternity, and if I were run over by a bus tomorrow I know I'd
rather people remembered me for having loved my neighbour as
myself than for having written one or two slightly interesting
books. I still write books, but the priorities are different. Or
rather, perhaps, an old priority has been reinforced.

How then does, or can, unemployment lead to positive
change? For most, unemployment is not chosen and it is a blow,

but new horizons may eventually open up. For some, what seem at first to be strategies of survival turn out to become a new and eventually treasured way of life. For such people, minority though they be, unemployment turns out to be a blessing in disguise. But the disguise is very effective for some time, and they would not call it a blessing at the time. Such was the experience of Rhona and Jim, for whom the first year of unemployment was traumatic indeed. After four years, though Jim still says he would take a job if it paid enough, he categorically asserts that unemployment has been a blessing for their family.

For a few, unemployment is chosen or accepted readily. Back in 1974, when my fixed-term job at Aberdeen University came to its natural end, I decided to do some writing for a few months financed by my savings. I discovered I was eligible for unemployment benefit, the few months extended into a couple of years, and I began to find myself thriving on the freedom and autonomy of my new working conditions. When after two such periods the local DHSS office started making life a bit tedious, some friends offered me some part-time building work, and so I became a self-employed author/builder, with the building effectively financing the writing. There was no major crisis, simply a natural progression to this state over a period of years from the starting point of a conventional academic career. I have no desire now to return to academic life. Had I had the debatable fortune of a tenured job in 1974, however, I would most likely still be in it now, not knowing what I'd missed.

Gerald also underwent an untraumatic transition. He had long fantasized about becoming self-employed, and probably never would have acted on his dream had his firm not made him redundant. He immediately set about getting advice about how to set up his dream firm and researching the market, as well as applying for conventional jobs, and — by a thin whisker — ended up with his firm. Three years later it is doing well, he told me as he gave me a lift in his new Rover. What is this fulfilled fantasy? Importing and marketing WCs! Well, everyone to his own dream.

For a few others the turning point comes first. Mike simply walked out of his job as a maintenance carpenter in Sheffield. A sensitive youth, he could stand no longer the hard and unfeeling atmosphere created by his mates at work. He was going with the girl next door who was at university and represented to Mike a way out of the poverty and harshness he had grown up in. After downing his tools he went for a long walk in the park and decided that he was henceforth going to open himself up to this world of new ideas and new feelings, so he went back and told his boss that he wasn't coming back. He did not sign on for the dole straightaway — instead, he went off to France to see his girlfriend — but effectively he became unemployed, because he wanted to turn his life in a new direction.

For many, of course, unemployment is neither a crisis nor an opportunity, but simply a part of an accepted way of life. For them, unemployment is a regular feature in a life of ill-paying, insecure or seasonal paid jobs.

New directions

There are perhaps three main, positive, new directions in which the unemployed person can go.

One is to a new career. Many of the unemployed do not move to an exciting new line of work, but downhill to similar work at a lower grade and wage, or downhill to less-skilled work. But a few find that a new and better form of work opens up. We have mentioned Samantha who in the end is delighted to have moved from radiography to selling houses. Or there are those clergymen who, unsuited to the work, have a nervous breakdown and, after a period on sickness or unemployment benefit, retrain and end up with a career in social work or engineering.

Then there is Alex, who runs the community workshop that

saved Jack and Marjorie's marriage. Alex had worked in the steel industry for thirty-eight years and was then made redundant. After five months on the dole, he was offered the job at the workshop, much to his surprise because he had never worked as a joiner and the workshop was largely tooled up for joinery. But he was one of those handymen who had turned his hand, even if only as an amateur, to just about everything, and was considered ideal for a workshop that included not just joinery but also a darkroom, a print-shop, and anything else for which there was both a local demand and money available.

Alex clearly loves this job, even though it pays much less than the steel industry. Not only can he use all his varied talents and interests, but also he loves the variety of the company. 'It's never the same from one day to the next. Not always the same little crew as in the works.' He is a good teacher, with great patience, and has a knack of defusing potential incidents. One black lad had been having some stick from the others, getting nudged just as he was about to make some delicate incision with his chisel; Alex just spent some time working alongside him and the other lads soon got the message to keep their distance. Alex is a boon to the workshop, and the workshop is a boon to him. Though he does not regret his days in the steel industry, he is surely ending his working life with the most satisfying job of all.

The second possibility is to move to self-employment. Starting up on your own is a risky business, and there are not many who give up a secure paid job for it. What you have to lose if you start from unemployment, though, may be considerably less than if you start from employment. As my period of unemployment lengthened and my chances of re-employment in academia receded, so I needed less and less courage to become self-employed. In fact, no courage at all: there came a point at which it was the only sensible next move.

The third possibility is to find a project that involves neither paid employment nor self-employment. Those who choose to be full-time parents are the most obvious example, though for unemployed women this may not be a new direction so much as choosing, or being forced, to go back to an old one. Unpaid community work is another one that, like fathering, can bring out the hitherto underdeveloped caring aspects of a man's character.

Poverty: trap or freedom?

In chapter 5, I described how poverty typically excludes a person from normal life in society. (That is why poverty levels differ from society to society. You need more money and resources to function in Britain than you do in rural India.) Poverty typically reduces your choices and opportunities, and the poverty of unemployment is no exception.

This has always been true, perhaps never more so than now when more and more of the tools of survival cost money and when most of us have lost the basic art, still more the opportunity, of getting by with little more than our hands and brains.

However, there has always been the experience of some that poverty leads not to a restricted life but to a new kind of freedom. Once St Francis had decided that the finery of his wealthy family was not for him and that he didn't care what people thought of him, then he was freed to do all kinds of things previously denied him. Pete, a modern day St Francis, finds the same. He can spend the day on the computer, writing a novel, going camping, just as he pleases. No one with a job or career has that kind of freedom. This is the freedom Marx looked forward to in his famous passage where he says, 'It is possible for me to do one thing today and another tomorrow, to hunt in the morning, fish in the afternoon, rear cattle in the evening, criticize after dinner, just as I have a mind'. As Pete puts it: 'I don't make plans; just see what turns up each day. I've got total freedom and total independence and no way would I give that up.' The result is a man who goes hungry if he runs out of money before his giro comes, but who can honestly say, 'I'm living a life of luxury'.

Pete reminds me also of Thoreau, the small-town American who for the two years 1845 — 7 lived off nature in the woods near his home, philosophizing about the freedom that results from spending as little time as possible producing the necessities of life.

Pete, like Thoreau and St Francis, is not married, and knows that marriage would spell the end of not only his freedom to please himself but also of his freedom to care for others. However, I have also met families for whom poverty has meant freedom. The dual-parent families one sometimes meets on the dole, like Rhona and Jim, have a freedom denied to the single-parent families that most with a working father have effectively become. Though Jim and Rhona are limited by money and resources, within these limits they are free to come and go as they please. A fine day can always be capitalized on; a sick child need not stop everyone else going out because there is always a spare parent to babysit; in particular the mother is free to have time off or by herself during the day. They are freed to handle their children well. If Rhona is coming to the end of her tether because the boys are being difficult, she can bow gracefully out and let Jim have a go. It usually works, she says.

During my academic career, my salary increased year by year due to promotion or increments up the scale. But, even though I was not married, my bank balance never got any healthier. What seemed to be happening was that, as a young man in my twenties, my lifestyle was automatically keeping pace with my peers: a car, a house, various consumer durables and fancy dinner parties all became a matter of course. This worried me a little: was I really in control of my own life? Could I ever manage on less if I had to?

The liberation provided by the first few months on the dole was partly that I realized that I could live on less, and comfortably too. From then on, the world began to open up, for I realized that, financially at least, I did not *need* a job and a career. Researching topics that interested me rather than topics given the imprimatur by the research councils then became possible.

With an absorbing project, money becomes less important.

I came to find that if you can live on the dole, or less, then you have a certain kind of power: the freedom both to choose to reject badly paid jobs that would involve selling your soul, and to choose to live in the non-formal economy according to your lights. It saddens me to see people accept an offer of a better-paying job that they know is less satisfying or of less use to humankind, or that they know involves moving house against the wishes of wife or children. That surely is the poverty of riches?

Suffering

Men and women of insight through the ages have perceived the two sides of poverty. Christianity has traditionally maintained the paradox that, though *poverty* is evil, *the poor* often find themselves blessed. This is so with other forms of suffering too, notably sickness and death, where the suffering soul may find some kind of personal resurrection, even in this life.

This is well understood in much modern work with cancer. There is the passionate belief that cancer is a scourge to be fought, and immense resources are put into finding a cure. At the same time, there is a mushrooming of hospices where the terminally ill can be helped to come to terms with their suffering. Reports are not rare of both the dying and those left behind finding some positive reorientation of their lives, even if only for the last few days. Hope and life can emerge even out of death. Certainly this is the positive message the Church has traditionally preached, even at the same time as it has trained doctors and agriculturists to fight sickness and death.

I fear, though, that recent pronouncements by church leaders on unemployment and poverty have lost this double edge. They join the clamour rightly proclaiming how evil unemployment is, but where is the message of hope and resurrection even in the midst of unemployment? Bishop David Sheppard, for example, in his book *Bias to the Poor* (Hodder and Stoughton 1983) talks of how poverty is evil because it reduces people's God-given ability to choose. But I could find no reference in the book to those poor, other than the ones who had chosen poverty, who have found it can open up new choices. Again, the recently formed Church Action on Poverty pressure group is concerned to get the Church on the side of the poor, which C.A.P. interprets as getting church-goers to join the poverty lobby. The poverty lobby, though, feels obliged to ignore the freedom and the power some find in poverty.

Why this lack of awareness of the paradoxical nature of poverty? Presumably those who are waging the political and educational battle against poverty think that any talk of the possibility of freedom in poverty will belittle the problem of poverty. They must suppose that what David Sheppard has called 'comfortable Britain' will hardly be convinced of the evil of poverty in Britain today if there is the slightest hint of the joys of poverty.

But I think this silence about the other side of poverty is wrong, for two reasons. It is morally wrong because it denies the possibility of hope for the unemployed. It is as cruel not to mention the signs of hope on the dole as it would be to ban all talk of those who have rediscovered themselves through sickness or other forms of suffering. This is not to say that you can give people hope simply by talking about it — we all know how unhelpful it is to say to the bereaved, 'Buck up, things could be worse!' People have to discover hope for themselves, in their own good time. But people will never know how to look for rainbows if, as in Orwell's newspeak, we have excised the word rainbow from the dictionary.

The other reason the silence is misguided is strategic. Fagin and Little are surely right when they argue that 'the more publicity that is given to the misery of unemployment, the more successful will [Mrs Thatcher's] policy be in persuading working people to accept low wage settlements and ensure a climate in which there is competition for the right to work.' Surely to argue, as I have done, that a man can lead a full life without paid work is to offer strength to the trade union movement. To ease the fear of unemployment gives courage to the employed as they face employers and governments who use unemployment as a threat. And the more who voluntarily withdraw from the labour force, the better will be the market position of those who do want paid work.

Hope and subversion

To tell of the occasional instance of freedom in poverty — with no money and no job — is more subversive yet. It is subversive because the establishment would have to admit that there is wisdom to be found among the poor. As one unemployed teenager, provocatively quoted in *Radio Times*, put it:

> They're sympathetic as long as you are portraying the right image of an unemployed person — and that is uptight, depressed, miserable and guilty. If you happen one day . . . to decide to put a defiant smile on your face, it's not my fault and why should I waste every minute of the day going insane over it, then they begin to doubt that you really care; and not to care about being unemployed is forbidden because that puts you on an equal footing with them.

It is disturbing also for the ordinary members of comfortable Britain to be told the big secret — that there are grown men leading a full life without a paid job. This is far from comfortable for the ordinary taxpayer, who wants his life of toil justified, not questioned and challenged by those his taxes support and who he feels should feel grateful.

It is even more disturbing to be told that some of those who have found a free and full life in relative poverty are precisely those castigated as fiddlers and petty criminals. But then that is how the authorities saw Jesus and some of the saints.

I have met people from the professional class who have chosen to work with the poor and the unemployed, and who have discovered wisdom and hope a-plenty there. Several of them do not want to return to their former comfortable lives, and I can see why. Not because they like do-gooding, but because there is so much more truth among the poor. I recall, when I did some research a dozen years ago on a school for delinquent boys, how struck I was by the basic honesty and straightforwardness of these children who had been committed there for 'dishonesty'. They were fundamentally more honest than the suburban children I had grown up with, not to mention less devious than the university who employed me to study them.

Those who try to get poverty and the pains of unemployment put on the Church's agenda usually try to stir up the conscience of comfortable Britain so that it feels responsible for the difficulties the poor are in. Whether through taxes or whatever, some more of our money has to end up with them. This is a little uncomfortable, and is what I attempted to do in Part Two.

Recently a vicar got two not-so-badly-off families to live at the supplementary benefit rate for a week, and to report back at the Harvest Festival service. One family had always kept tight control of their budget, and managed all right. The other family was more typical in that it tried hard and failed. They cancelled going to see their grown-up son for the weekend because of course they had 'sold' the car, they cancelled the newspapers and made other cuts, and still ran out of money by Thursday. This family now confidently gives a few pounds every week to the parish worker to give to anyone on supplementary benefit she knows to be in difficulty. This family has become a St Martin, cutting off a bit of its cloak each week to give to the beggar, while remaining comfortably seated on its white charger. To become St Martins to the poor on their doorstep would be a vast step forward for most churches and for many families.

What is usually omitted is to show that the poor have things to teach *us*, that what we can receive from the poor is as important as what they can receive from us. That is *very* uncomfortable. In the words of David Jenkins, Bishop of Durham, who like the poor has had his own measure of vilification, 'the poor and the marginals are not primarily objects of charity and compassion, but rather subjects and agents of the judgement of God and pointing to the ways of the kingdom'. That is from his book *The Contradiction of Christianity* (SCM Press 1976); clearly he understands the paradox of poverty. It is hard enough to act as St Martin; it is harder still to cope with meeting a St Francis who has found freedom in poverty and who challenges our whole way of life in which worth is bought by money, and money by a paid job.

As one radical Glasgow minister recently put it to me, what is needed is not a church for the poor, but a church of the poor.

11 Ways Forward

My researches with the unemployed have uncovered two things. Part Two shows that our society sadistically removes most of their opportunities to contribute to society. How then can society alter its treatment of the unemployed? Part Three shows that there are many unemployed who have not given up but are struggling to live a decent life against the odds, and a few who have used unemployment to escape from wage slavery into a more positive life. How then may unemployment be turned into a gateway to new pastures for more than just the self-selected few?

Modest reforms

In addition to creating new jobs, there are several things that can be done to make life far better for both the employed and for the unemployed. These modest reforms need not challenge the paid-work ethic that the establishment clings to so tenaciously.

Work sharing. If more people want paid work than there is paid work to go around, then natural justice indicates that the available work must be shared around more equally. Those currently with paid work must be prepared to work shorter hours. If there is economic growth, this increased spare time will take the place of a rise in real wages; if the economy is not growing, then the shorter hours will have to be at the old hourly rate and real take-home pay will go down. If as a country we have to make a sacrifice to go through the present recession, then this clearly is the sacrifice that is most just for the whole community.

This solution is most just for the unemployed, because it is paid work in the formal economy that they overwhelmingly desire. Every single survey into the attitudes of the unemployed in the present recession has shown a large majority both wanting and seeking good paid work. After all, power, prestige and status come from money, and money comes from a wage. All the money the unemployed receive goes into physical subsistence, and there is none left to enable them to play a part in the community. It is no wonder they become second-class citizens.

There is considerable evidence that many paid workers would prefer more leisure to more money. *The Times* survey of 23 June 1980 showed this, and betrays glimpses of a grudging acceptance by the establishment that the supposed British disease of not wanting to work very hard may well be an asset rather than a liability if it can be translated into shorter hours. The 1984 coal miners' strike has as one of its aims the establishment of a four-day week for miners, surely a rational move if the Coal Board wants to reduce the man hours it has to pay for, and if miners want to retain their jobs. And surely, whatever camaraderie is generated down the pit, miners have always wanted more of the fresh air above.

The main problems with sharing out the work more equally have to do with practical and political anxieties of both workers and management. Unions want shorter hours but not if it means less pay. Also they are rightly concerned about any move to replace full-time labour (unionized, male, with good conditions and security) with part-timers (usually female, difficult to unionize, and with non-existent security). The Tories' *job splitting* scheme has attracted considerable hostility for this and other reasons.

Job sharing is rather different. It involves two people sharing the same job and deciding between themselves how to divide up the hours, workload, pensions and so on. Job sharing is sometimes resisted by employers who imagine it will be administratively inconvenient for them, though the evidence is that two people sharing a job are usually more productive than one. Job sharing can be of particular value to women who want the benefits of a full-time job (such as interest, using their

185

qualifications and skills, and good conditions) but want only to work part-time. It also has great potential for men who want to combine a career in paid work with a career in fathering.

Another form of work sharing which we have seen can work successfully is rotating lay-offs. Instead of making some of the workforce redundant, workers are all laid off in rotation for a specified number of weeks in agreement with the unions. This replaces the dead end of redundancy for some of the workforce by sabbaticals for all of the workforce.

Work sharing makes sense for virtually everyone. However, it involves asking industrial relations (which often are not good in Britain) to cope with problems (unemployment and the future of work) which governments and ordinary individual taxpayers are ducking at every available opportunity. Workers and managers negotiating work-sharing agreements need all the encouragement and support they can get.

More resources for the unemployed. Meanwhile, the unemployed are still with us. Until there is paid work for them in the formal economy, it is essential for the health of our society that they be released for creative informal activity. That means the immediate implementation of one or more of the simple changes in the supplementary benefit scales, as outlined at the end of chapter 9: entitling the long-term unemployed to the long-term supplementary benefit rate; making the earnings rule less onerous; and adding an 'investment quota' to the other basic needs such as food, clothing and heating on which social security rates are calculated.

More taxation. This will add to costs, a little. It should be paid for by those in paid work, either through increased income tax or increased national insurance contributions. If we are not willing to share out the paid work more fairly, then people with paid work should be willing to pay enough benefit to the unemployed to enable them to work informally. As it is, we in

186

Britain are not particularly highly taxed compared with other countries.

The low paid, however, should not be expected to pay any of this extra tax, otherwise there will be a worsening of the present scandal in which some of the low paid have less disposable income than some of the unemployed: a major cause of ill feeling both toward and by the unemployed. Already the low paid in Britain pay more tax than in virtually any other country.

A radical reform

A much more radical reform is based on two realizations: that people understand paid work to be a mixed blessing, incurring personal pain as well as financial gain; and that it is an unfounded myth that people will necessarily descend into sloth and inactivity if they do not need to earn a living. It is radical in that the paid work ethic held by the establishment is challenged. But it is realistic in that it is based on ordinary life for millions of people in Britain today and on how they feel about it. More than our present system of work incentives, it is in tune with people's ambivalent feelings about work.

Basically, what is proposed is that members of a civilized, prosperous, advanced industrial society such as ours have *the right not to engage in paid work* as well as the right to engage in it. And if there is not enough paid work to go around, we need our heads examining if we do not give people that right.

In a recent TV discussion, someone said that there are only two ways of solving unemployment: creating more paid jobs, or changing the work ethic that makes people want paid jobs. Len Murray, Secretary of the TUC, was asked which he preferred. He replied, jobs first, and then we can work toward changing attitudes. I agree with Mr Murray that it is not easy to change attitudes, probably not as easy as providing more paid work. However, the fact is that already there are many in Britain whose adherence to the paid work ethic is no more than lukewarm to say the least. It will take some years to get three million more jobs in Britain, whoever is running the country; it would take less than a day to find three million people who'd rather not have to work for a living, at least for a while. The tragedy is that those three million are not in the main the same three million who are unemployed. We have millions out of paid work who'd like a paid job; and millions who have to go out to work to support their families, when there are equally constructive things they'd rather be doing. To be able to devise things so that those without paid work are the ones who don't want it is surely within the capabilities of a civilization capable of sending people to the moon?

Arranging this could be simple. What is required is a social security system called the social dividend. This has also gone under other names, such as a national dividend, guaranteed minimum income or negative income tax. I have given a much more detailed description of it in my book *Fair Shares* but — put simply — this is how it works:

Everyone apart from those in prison and psychiatric hospital are given by the state an amount of money sufficient to live on. This *means everyone* — all women, children, pensioners, and others without a paid job, and all with a paid job. This 'social dividend' is set at about the current supplementary benefit rate and is paid for by income tax of around 60 per cent on every pound earned; *all* allowances against tax are abolished. It also abolishes virtually the whole of the present complicated social security system (including pensions and the forty-plus different means-tested benefits), national insurance contributions by both employee and employer, and some present income tax.

An individual's net income will be his or her social dividend plus any earnings, minus income tax. Those currently unemployed will have much the same income as at present, but there is no earnings rule. They can earn money just like anyone else, and are taxed just like anyone else.

Those individuals with a full-time paid job will pay roughly twice in income tax what they receive in social dividend, so will be rather worse off. However, any dependants will have their own social dividend. A family with the same number of dependants as full-time paid workers will therefore experience little or no change in net household income. Those with more dependants than paid workers will be better off.

As far as employment and unemployment are concerned, the effects of the social dividend would be startling. Our present arrangements make it profitable (usually) either to have a full-time paid job, or to be on social security, but grossly discourages anything in between. Likewise, employers have to pay a living wage, or not get the job done; all other work is done in the household and informal economies and is not paid (the one exception being the black economy); because of this a lot of work simply is not done. This is very far from a free market for labour, and is neither a humane nor an efficient way of getting things done.

The social dividend is the *only* way in which the market can be freed, because it disconnects wages from the need to subsist. Everyone is freed to engage in paid work as much or as little as he or she desires, trade unionists are freed from the spectre of a wage too low to live on, and employers are freed to pay the market rate for the job. Most people currently in paid work would want to continue in it, either because they enjoy it or because they want the money. But those who would rather retire from paid work and do other things are enabled to do so, without any stigma. Part-time work would increase.

If there is the remotest possibility of Britain developing into a high-technology economy in which, say, only 10 per cent of the population are required in the few highly automated paid jobs, then it is crucial that we work toward easing the present antagonism between taxpayers and claimants. Otherwise, there will be more and more claimants dependent on fewer and fewer rich earners who will not give away their earnings lightly. Under a social dividend scheme, the distinction between paid employment and unemployment would simply vanish. The division between taxpayers and claimants would be greatly diminished if not abolished because everyone receives the social dividend and is a claimant, while many of those currently unemployed would be in paid work at least a few hours a week and would be taxpayers.

Some kind of social dividend scheme is the *only* way to abolish totally the poverty and unemployment traps in which net income does not rise as wages rise and in which the low paid have less net income than some of the unemployed. In a social dividend scheme, all paid work is rewarded, whether you are at the top or the bottom of the income ladder. The basis for the resentment of the low paid toward the unemployed would therefore be removed at root. Further, the social dividend is the only way in which a high-technology future with a mass release from paid work could possibly lead to leisure rather than the trap of poverty for all those released.

The haunting spectre of unemployment would be automatically removed. The pressure to be in paid work, however grim or soul-less, will be removed, and people will be freed to act on their feelings about work. With the pressure off the low-paid, there will be less or no bigotry from them toward those who choose to work at non-paying activities. It will then become possible to face a future of declining opportunities for paid work, safe in the knowledge that the basis for resentment and bitterness has been removed. We could then face the future as a united community, rather than as the increasingly divided two nations that we are becoming. Surely other things will still divide us, but we will have removed those divisions based on work and its current crazy distribution.

Objections

There have been several varieties of social dividend proposed on both sides of the Atlantic and on both sides of the political spectrum; and even more objections to the proposals. The objections focus around the feeling that social dividend schemes are utopian and unworkable, and that the most that can be said for them is that they are ahead of their time. That, however, is precisely what the social dividend is not. Let's look at some of the objections.

Discipline. One objection is that it is fine for Tony Walter or some other academic to talk of being freed to use our time creatively and actively, but most people do not have the education or intelligence to be trusted to use their time purposefully, were it returned to them. In other words, you can't trust the working class. (The otherwise enlightened Thoreau thought likewise, 'The vast majority of men require the discipline of labor which enslaves them for their good.' They could not be trusted with the leisure that he, Thoreau, had made such enlightened use of. Not much change in 150 years.)

This objection is unadulterated, sexist piffle. The people who make this objection are often the very same who say that women should be at home looking after their children. In other words, poorly educated working-class girls can be trusted to work without pay, for a hundred hours a week, without supervision, but boys need the discipline of wage labour if they are not to descend into sloth and indolence.

It is usually men who make the objection, for women know perfectly well that millions of them already work hard not for a wage but for a (sometimes flimsy) guarantee of subsistence. I am not wanting to justify the conditions of housework, but simply to point out that women at least do not need the discipline of wage labour in order to work. Why then do the male critics have such little faith in the ability of their own sex to work autonomously and without external direction? Are they correct? If, heaven help my sex, they are, then surely what we have to do is to educate both boys and girls not for work, not for leisure, not for motherhood, but for autonomous action, so that they can become adults in control of their own lives, lives which are fulfilling and contribute to the community. To continue to insist on wage slavery as the only way of making boys into civilized human beings (and doubtless some managers who want a quiescent and malleable workforce will continue to insist on this) is nothing short of barbarous.

Power in the family. Objection number two also comes from men. Schemes where each individual, rather than each household, is entitled to a social dividend will mean that some of the transfer of cash from earners to dependants that currently takes place voluntarily within the private family will happen automatically. Married women without paid work will no longer be the grateful vassals of earning husbands who decide in their generosity and love to 'give' the wife some housekeeping and perhaps a little more. Most earners will surely continue to give some of their earnings to others in their household, but no longer will these others be totally dependent for life and succour on a man dishing out either a wage or social security benefit. This is the price men will have to pay for being freed from *having* to go out to work to support their families.

This is a book about unemployment, not relations between men and women, so I cannot go further into the obviously major implications of the social dividend for family life. Suffice it to point out, as has Anne Miller of Heriot-Watt University, that this objection does not make the social dividend impractical politically. Though men hold political power in our society, women have more than half the votes. Moreover, husbands with large family responsibilities are also likely to vote for a system that increases net family income and takes some of the pressure off them to work overtime. It is net disposable household income that many men will be concerned about, and for at least half of the country's households this would go up under a social dividend scheme.

Power of the wage. Objection number three points out that social security benefits are vulnerable to being cut. Anyone who chooses to live on the social dividend alone will be vulnerable to the real value of the dividend being eroded, and only those with a wage will have any power to maintain the value of their income. Only a wage provides power, and therefore policy should be directed toward increasing paid employment, not enabling people to opt out of it.

This is a curious objection. It conveniently forgets that over half of the British population do not earn a wage anyway, so it presumably would have to go along with the more extreme feminists who demand a wage for housework, and indeed a wage for schoolwork also, if women and children are not to be exploited by husbands and fathers in the home. Or else, it will have to assume that some magic benevolence comes over wage-earners when they enter their own front door and are confronted by dependants without the protection of a wage. There surely is considerable evidence that the abuse of the powerless occurs within homes on a large scale.

So, once it is agreed that children, pensioners, the sick and many women, do not and never will have the protection of their own wage packet, then we see that all the social dividend does is to place the currently unemployed in a financial position similar to these other groups, for whom subsistence is guaranteed (by their pension or their parents or their husband). The social dividend in fact *increases* the relative power of those without a wage because it makes them less dependent on potentially unreliable personal relations.

But you ask, are the state and the taxpayer to be trusted to maintain the value of the social dividend? Yes, because every family receives dividends, and everyone has an interest in maintaining its value. This is an important strength of a system that makes everyone into claimants. (There is a problem here, however, if the dividend shows up in the government's accounts as an expenditure, for governments are usually committed to reducing public expenditure. The advantage of arranging the dividend as a negative income tax is that it shows up in Whitehall's accounts as reduced taxation, which looks better to a government committed to lowering both taxation and expenditure.)

As important, the social dividend would be the most creative force imaginable for encouraging work sharing. With the dichotomy between full-time paid work and unemployment abolished, and wage levels freed, many of the pressures against sharing out work more equally will be gone. Indeed, the freeing of the labour market may well lead to more rather than fewer jobs.

Wage levels. Trade unionists may object that the social dividend will bring some wage levels down. True. But if net household income is what people are really concerned with, then wage levels will be seen to be not the sole determining factor in one's standard of living.

Bureaucracy. Some objectors recoil in horror at so much of the national cake being dished out by the state. But the bureaucracy required to operate such a simple system would be far less than currently operates the social security system; and because the social dividend would unite income tax with social security, the prying of the state into private lives in order to determine eligibility for means-tested benefits would end for good.

Some object that dependent wives would prefer to have their housekeeping given them by their husband than by a state allowance. The only precedent to date, however, indicates otherwise. In the 1970s, women pressed for, and have subsequently welcomed, the shift from a child tax allowance benefiting the husband, which he could choose whether to pass on to mother or child, to a cash benefit payable directly to the mother. The social dividend is a citizen benefit analogous to child benefit. It operates on similar principles and would be as simple to operate as this widely accepted benefit.

Cost. A superficial glance suggests that the social dividend would be enormously expensive. In fact, it is not. Though a radical idea, the social dividend or negative income tax would be cheaper (in government accounting terms) than my ideologically more modest proposal of increasing benefits. This is because the social dividend frees people to work in order to top up their dividend; in other words, the extra cash that the poor require will come more readily from their own labour rather than from the exchequer.

The New Right is committed both to freeing people to work and reducing government expenditure. A negative income tax could well achieve both these ends, and in addition support the poor more effectively than does our present system of social security. Negative income tax/social dividend is a practical scheme worthy of the attention of both free marketeers and those who have long cherished the welfare state.

From hassle to freedom

Many radical writers have understood that some people should be released with dignity from paid work. However, each writer usually specifies *who* should be released for *what,* and there is little consensus among them.

The commonest suggestion is that early retirement should be encouraged, combined with increasing opportunities for the young to find paid employment. Certainly many older workers would like to retire early from unpleasant or unhealthy work, and there is widespread anxiety that the young will never learn good habits on the dole. Roger Clarke, worried that the young should not 'miss out on the socializing aspects of the discipline of paid employment', advocates this combination in his book *Work in Crisis* (St Andrew Press 1982, p. 132).

Others have proposed that, since it is the parents of young families who have to work hardest in both formal and household economies, it is at this stage in the life-cycle that people should be released from paid work. If the average person is going to be unemployed for three or four years in their lifetime, it is sensible that they should take this spare time when they most need it. So it is possible to argue for paid maternity and paternity leave, which if generous enough, could virtually abolish unemployment. Young parents of both sexes could voluntarily withdraw from the workforce, releasing jobs for those with more time to do them.

A third possibility for which, like paternity leave, I have considerable sympathy, is that those unemployed who can show they are engaged in voluntary work or other worthwhile activity would receive a higher rate of benefit and be released from some of the onerous conditions of signing on. Such has been argued by Michael Moynagh, former CBI adviser on pay policy and unemployment.[1]

The trouble with all these well-intentioned proposals, though, is that they are profoundly paternalistic. They understand that people must be freed to work, but only those people specified by the system or its enlightened advisers. So, the old can be released but not the young. Parents but not the single. The voluntary worker but not, perhaps, the motorbike tinkerer. Imagine the bizarre rules that would be developed for social security clerks to operate Moynagh's suggestion that they should have the power to determine whether an unemployed youth is using his time wisely!

One of the key experiences of being unemployed is hassle. Unlike the paid worker, you are not allowed to lead your life as you and your family see fit, but are subject to rules and to officials specifying what you can and cannot do. Your life has to fit into what the system specifies. Your private life is breached by the public gaze of the social security official. The rules and attitudes that sentence the unemployed to passivity may be summed up in this one word: hassle.

The problems with any proposal attempting to free just the old, parents or the altruistic from the paid work ethic is that it will bring with it more hassle, the opposite of freedom. Many will still not 'fit': the single person who wants paid leave not to look after a baby but to look after a frail mother or a sick uncle, the youth who does not want a paid job, the sixty-year-old who does, the unemployed person working busily at a 'non-approved'

[1] Reported in *Christian Arena*, March 1984, p. 39.

occupation. They will still experience hassle in trying to persuade the system to support them.

The social dividend is the only proposal I have come across that really does free both the employed and the unemployed to lead creative lives in whichever of the four economies they choose, to the benefit of both themselves and the community. Just now, many of the unemployed are sentenced to idleness, while many of the employed are sentenced to slavery. Both sentences can be reprieved.

12 How the Book Was Written

About ten years ago I began to feel that there was something not quite right about the official views of unemployment, nor about the accounts provided by social scientists and other commentators. It all began when I myself was first unemployed. I soon became aware that my personal experience of unemployment was not what it was supposed to be, according to the well-meant brochures given me by counselling services for the unemployed, or according to the occasional report from the dole queue in *New Society*, both of which portrayed unemployment as an inevitable slide into despair. For me, it was just the opposite: a time of personal liberation. I kept my counsel, though. I thought that, being a voluntarily unemployed house-owning academic, I must surely be in a rather unusual and privileged position. But over the years since then I have come across person after person, right across the social spectrum, who has reported similar experiences.

Also I began to sense a conspiracy of silence among social scientists, journalists and politicians on both the Left and the Right as to the possibility that there might indeed be life after unemployment, though it may be common knowledge down at the local pub.

I began to feel the whole matter should be brought out into the open, and was encouraged in this by one or two friends. I began to wonder: are there particular family or financial circumstances which make it easier to live actively without a paid job? Is it easier for the single or the married? For the rich or for the poor? For the young or for the middle aged? In areas of high or of low unemployment? I began to read some of the studies that had already been made of the unemployed, and in particular I began to read between the lines, wondering for example about the 8 per cent whose health improved in studies exposing how 'bad' unemployment is for your health. I looked for the signs of hope and creativity in case studies which deny any hope for the unemployed outside of finding them paid work. I found that, not seeking hope, authors simply did not see the hope in their own material. I thought carefully about my own unemployment and asked my friends about when they had been unemployed.

I was a little concerned that the picture that was emerging was based largely on the south of England and on the middle classes, so I went on a week's tour of the major conurbations of industrial Yorkshire and Merseyside, seeking people from a very different social background who were also finding life on the dole enjoyable, or at least tolerable. They turned out to be a fair cross-section of skilled, semi-skilled and unskilled working class men, and — along with my middle-class acquaintances from the south — theirs are the lives on which this book is based. I met them without difficulty through a few contacts who lived in inner city areas and were involved in community work, local politics or the Church.

It is a very small group, and far from being random or representative — about twenty people. But it seems to me to have validity as evidence for the case I have argued, and which I summarize here:

1 If those who enjoy life on the dole are as tiny a minority as is often supposed by those to the left of centre, then why did I find it so easy to meet them in a week of wandering around cities I did not know well? Why did the local workers I used as contacts immediately recognize what I was on about, and could immediately introduce me to the characters who now people the pages of this book?

2 The reader may rest assured that the twenty or so unemployed people who appear in the pages of this book have not been judiciously selected from a much larger sample of people met, of whom the twenty are unrepresentative. Indeed, virtually every person I met has found their way into this book.

3 Almost every one of those I met, both unemployed in the

north and previously unemployed friends in the south, fit my thesis that unemployment can be a blessing in disguise. Certainly there are many I was not seeking who have found unemployment an unmitigated disaster and a dead end; but surely it casts doubts on the conventional 'disaster' thesis that among those I met I did not find *any* who fitted it!

4   As mentioned in the first chapter, there needs to be only one case of someone enjoying unemployment to disprove the popular notion that unemployment itself causes emotional, personal, financial or any other kind of problems. The few who thrive on unemployment, however few they be, can tell us a great deal. In social science, as in natural science, the one exception to the rule can often tell us a lot more then the ninety-nine who obey the rule. Once a rule has been discovered (for example, that unemployment is painful), then it is the exceptions that advance our knowledge further.

I was looking for those for whom unemployment is an unmitigated success. I did not find many of them. What I did find were many for whom it has been a mixed blessing. What emerged more and more clearly was that the negative aspects of their experience of unemployment are not inevitable, and are largely the result of society's attitudes and policies, as I have described them in Part Two. Unless you draw a really enormous sample, no sample of the unemployed can claim to be representative. People experience unemployment so variously that there is no such thing as the typical unemployed person. Many articles and books are written as though there were. *He* is usually assumed to be a middle-aged man redundant from a declining traditional heavy industry. So an interview with an unemployed shipyard worker on Tyneside gets written up as an article about 'the plight of the unemployed'.

Rather than attempting to find this mythical creature, I have tried to add some new dimensions to a hitherto rather monochrome picture of unemployment. You do not need a representative sample to do that.

One or two other queries about this method of gathering evidence are perhaps more to the point. Many of the people I met in their own homes. Adrian Sinfield points out in his book *What Unemployment Means* (p. 41) that the place of interview can affect what people talk about. At home in front of the family, the unemployed breadwinner tends to talk more of the material deprivations of unemployment; it is outside the benefit office or in the pub among male company that he is more likely to talk of being degraded as a man. Sinfield also found that only after they have regained paid work do some men talk of their anger and depression while unemployed. Maybe I'd have got a different picture had I met people as they walk out of the dole office (which is how some researchers of the unemployed draw their samples), or in the local pub?

Maybe. If so, then how to fit together a picture say of despond outside the social security office, but optimism from the same person at home? For the man who is being excluded from the formal economy but is finding new roles in the household or informal economies, it would not be surprising if he felt and expressed his loss outside the dole office, the point of contact with the formal world of paid work; nor surprising that he would be optimistic in kitchen or potting shed where he is finding new interests. If people are experiencing a process of crucifixion and resurrection, then we would expect a sense of loss to persist in those areas where it is most acutely felt, and transcended in the areas where new opportunities are opening up.

Though the chance method I employed in finding creatively unemployed people in no way invalidates the argument of this book, it does raise some unanswered questions. Those I met are not typical of the unemployed in terms of age, race and sex. They are mainly aged 25—45, with youth unemployment and elderly redundancy under-represented:

Teenagers	3
20s	4
30s	7
40s	4
50s	–
60s	2
	20

Thirteen are married, and seven single. There is only one black person. The most glaring oddity is that there are only three women, and two of these were positive about unemployment only as a transition to a new career; all three I already knew as friends.

One of the problems of meeting people through the method I adopted is that it is difficult interpreting the untypicality of those met. Is it simply due to the chance process of encountering them (there may be lots of creatively unemployed black women in their 50s but I just didn't happen across them), or did I tend to meet white males in their prime because the creatively unemployed *are* usually white males in their prime? The issue is most pertinent in the case of the absent women. I asked my contacts some such question as 'I'm looking for people who do not seem to find unemployment a problem. Do you know any?' Why did they introduce me to no women? Because unemployed women tend to be invisible, with their friends assuming they've fitted back into the kitchen and therefore not defining them as unemployed? Or because even fewer women than men have found resurrection through unemployment?

This book has been able to identify the things that aid creative unemployment — money, resources, opportunities in the non-formal economies, and flexibility concerning what is a man's and what a woman's work. What I have not been able to identify is whether some people are more likely than others to stumble on to these things. More research would be needed to answer that. In the meantime, it is quite clear what has to be done if more people are to turn a public tragedy into some kind of personal triumph.

Further Reading

This list includes most of the works by the authors mentioned in the text, plus some other reading.

Introduction

Dauncey, G., *The Unemployment Handbook*, National Extension College 1982.

Chapter 1

WORK

Burns, S., *The Household Economy*, Beacon Press (Boston) 1976.

Gershuny, J., *After Industrial Society?*, Macmillan 1978.

Handy, C., *The Future of Work*, Blackwell 1984.

Henry, S., *The Hidden Economy*, Martin Robertson 1978.

Henry, S., 'The Working Unemployed', *Sociological Review*, 30(3), 1982, pp. 460–77.

Kumar, K., '"Unemployment" as a Problem in the Development of Industrial Societies', *Sociological Review*, 32(2), 1984, pp. 185–233.

Oakley, A., *The Sociology of Housework*, Martin Robertson 1974.

Pahl, R., *Divisions of Labour*, Blackwell 1984.

Robertson, J., 'Breakdown or Breakthrough', *The Ecologist*, Nov. 1977, pp. 340–8.

Rothwell, S., 'Women and Work', *Resurgence*, 86, May/June 1981.

Work and Society Newsletter, 56 Britton Street, London EC1M 5NA. Quarterly.

Chapter 2

THE WORK ETHIC

Anthony, P. D., *The Ideology of Work*, Tavistock 1978.

Arendt, H., *The Human Condition*, University of Chicago Press 1958.

Bleakley, D., *Work: The Shadow and the Substance*, SCM 1983.

Pahl, R., 'Family, Community and Unemployment', *New Society*, 21 Jan. 1982.

Rose, M., *Reworking the Work Ethic*, Batsford 1985.

Thompson, E. P., 'Time, Work-Discipline and Industrial Capitalism', *Past and Present*, 38, 1967, pp. 56—97.

Wiener, M., *English Culture and the Decline of the Industrial Spirit 1850—1980,* Cambridge University Press 1981.

Chapter 3

POLICIES AND STATISTICS

Beveridge, W., *Social Insurance and Allied Services*, HMSO 1942.

Donnison, D., *The Politics of Poverty,* Martin Robertson 1982.

Employment Gazette, Department of Employment. Monthly.

Rimmer, L. and Popay, J., *Employment Trends and the Family,* Study Commission on the Family, 1982.

Unemployment Unit Bulletin, 9 Poland Street, London W1V 3DG.

Chapter 4

THE POLITICS OF RIGHTEOUSNESS

Cohen, S., *Folk Devils and Moral Panics*, MacGibbon & Kee 1972.

Duncan, H. D., *Communication and Social Order,* Oxford University Press 1968.

Golding, P. and Middleton, S., *Images of Welfare*, Martin Robertson 1982.

Holman, R., *Poverty,* Martin Robertson 1978.

Runciman, W. G., *Relative Deprivation and Social Justice*, Routledge 1966.

Chapters 5 and 6

EXPERIENCES OF UNEMPLOYMENT

Coyle, A., *Redundant Women,* Women's Press 1984.

Fagin, L. and Little, M., *The Forsaken Families,* Penguin 1984.

McKee, L. and Bell, C., 'His Unemployment: Her Problem', in S. Allen (ed.), *The Experience of Unemployment,* Macmillan 1985.

McKenna, S. and Fryer, D., 'Perceived Health During Lay-Off and Early Retirement', *Occupational Health*, 36(5), May 1984, pp. 201—6.

Marsden, D., *Workless,* Croom Helm 1982.

Morris, L., 'Renegotiation of the Domestic Division of Labour', in H. Newby (ed.), *Restructuring Capital*, Macmillan 1985.

Seabrook, J., *Unemployment,* Quartet 1982.

Sinfield, A., *What Unemployment Means,* Martin Robertson 1981.

THE PSYCHOLOGY OF UNEMPLOYMENT

Jahoda, M., *Employment and Unemployment,* Cambridge University Press 1982.

Jahoda, M. *et al., Marienthal,* Tavistock 1972 (first published 1933).

Warr, P., 'Work, Jobs and Unemployment', *Bulletin of the British Psychological Society*, 36, 1983, pp. 305—11.

Chapters 7—10

HOPE

Dauncey, G., *Nice Work If You Can Get It,* National Extension College 1983.

Fryer, D. and Payne, R., 'Pro-Active Behaviour in Unemployment', *Leisure Studies*, 3, 1984, pp. 273—95.

Illich, I., *The Right to Useful Unemployment*, Marion Boyars 1979.

Initiatives, Centre for Employment Initiatives, 140A Gloucester Mansions, Cambridge Circus, London WC2H 8PA. Quarterly.

Roberts, K. *et al.,* 'Youth Unemployment: an old problem or a new life-style?', *Leisure Studies,* 1, 1982, pp. 171—82.

Schumacher, E. F., *Small Is Beautiful*, Abacus 1974.

Chapter 11

THE SOCIAL DIVIDEND

Ashby, P., *Social Security After Beveridge*, Bedford Square Press 1984.

Collard, D., 'Social Dividend and Negative Income Tax', ch. 11 in C. Sandford *et al., Taxation and Social Policy*, Heinemann 1980.

Roberts, K., *Automation, Unemployment and the Distribution of Income,* European Centre for Work and Society 1982.
Walter, J. A., *Fair Shares?*, Handsel 1985.

Church organizations

Church Action on Poverty, 27 Blackfriars Road, Salford M3 7AQ.
Church Action with the Unemployed, 146 Queen Victoria Street, London EC4V 4BY.

Both these organizations provide information on responses to unemployment.